THE
MANCHESTER UNITED

BOOK OF LISTS

DEDICATION

This book is dedicated to my wife Janice and our two sons, Marc and Paul.

ACKNOWLEDGEMENTS

I wish to thank the following people for giving me ideas on various lists for this book: Barry Moorhouse of Manchester United, John Dempsey and Wilson Steele of Carryduff Manchester United Supporters Club, Adam Bostock, Addy Dearnaley and Philip Crummy. I want to say a special thank you to Alex Ferguson for his help and encouragement. I think it is fitting that I pay tribute to my Mum and Dad for everything they have done for me. I would also like to say a special thank you to my wife, Janice, who spent many hours proofreading the book for me and for the endless support she provided when I was working on the book. Finally, another special thank you goes to my sons for all their help.

To have one book published about Manchester United is a dream for a United fan. To have two books published is even beyond my wildest dreams. I am quite proud to have achieved this because I am just an ordinary fan. I hope you enjoy reading the book. Perhaps you will find something out about our great club.

Chalkie

LIST OF ABBREVIATIONS

EC	European Cup (or European Champions' Cup)
ECC	European Champions' Cup (or European Cup)
ECL	European Champions' League
ECWC	European Cup-Winners' Cup
FAC	FA Cup
FLC	Football League Cup
FR	Friendly game
ICFC	Inter Cities Fairs Cup
PFA	Professional Footballers' Association
P W D L	Played Won Drew Lost
QF	Quarter-final
QR	Qualifying round
SF	Semi-final
R	Round
UEFA	UEFA Cup
WCC	World Club Championship
(a)	Away game
(h)	Home game
(n)	Neutral venue
(W)	Wembley Stadium
aet	After Extra Time
agg	Aggregate score
a	Away Leg of Cup game
h	Home Leg of Cup game
h and a	Home and Away Legs of Cup game
Div. 1	English League Division 1 (First Division)
Div. 2	English League Division 2 (Second Division)
Div. 3	English League Division 3 (Third Division)
pens	Penalties
Sub	Substitute
TM	Test matches (played 1893-97)

THE MANCHESTER UNITED
BOOK OF LISTS

Foreword by EAMONN HOLMES

Compiled by JOHN WHITE

First published in 1999 by Manchester United Books
An imprint of
Andre Deutsch
76 Dean Street
London W1V 5HA

HYPERLINK http://www.vci.co.uk

Cover and pages designed by Design 23

Printed and bound by Butler and Tanner, Frome and London

A catalogue record for this book is available from the British Library

ISBN 0 233 99616 8

PICTURE ACKNOWLEDGEMENTS
COVER PHOTOS:
Action Images, Colorsport, Sporting Pictures, London Features
INSIDE PHOTOS:
Action Images: 9, 18a, 18b, 98, 103, 108, 111, 147, 155;
Action Plus: 23, 106, 113, 146, 163;
Colorsport: 5, 17, 29, 32, 41, 44, 120, 133, 154;
Empics: 11, 39, 139;
MEN: 66, 73;
Popperfoto: 59, 139;
Sporting Pictures: 26, 30, 40, 48, 55, 72, 129;
Capital Pictures: 7

Contents

FOREWORD BY
EAMONN HOLMES

I've found football to be an amazing common denominator. Working on telly, I meet an amazing array of people and have to attend so many functions. Sometimes, it has to be said, the going is tough. Conversation doesn't always flow and it's at times like these that I fall back on football. When this happens, colleagues or other people in my company, roll their eyes with that sort of 'Oh no – here he goes again' look. I guarantee though, within seconds they are smiling in disbelief as I strike gold. I have talked football with this Prime Minister and the previous one, this Chancellor of the Exchequer and the previous one, with pop stars, clergy and film stars. But most of all I love talking football with my children.

If you are a parent you don't need me to tell you there are only a few things you can really have in common with your children and it is unlikely that these will include fashion, music or politics. But with football you talk the same language, whether you support the same team or not. 'Who will he pick today?' 'Why doesn't he make a substitution?' 'I'd buy him – what do you think?' 'That ref needs glasses.' Talking points are what football is all about and this book provides talking points in abundance.

Because I talk about football quite a lot on the box people will often say, 'You're a football fanatic aren't you?' The truth is I'm not. I'm a football fan but not a fan-atic. No, the author of this book is though.

John White is an amazingly dedicated man. An accident of birth has meant his surname refers to the wrong colour. John 'White' should really be called John 'Red' – such is his devotion to and knowledge of Manchester United. Actually I think John should keep his surname, but get a new middle name by deed poll. I think John White should become John 'Red' and White! When you read this book you will know why. John has researched every list you need to know, and quite a few you don't need to know about the mighty Reds.

For John White supporting Manchester United is not an option – it's an addiction! And you'll be addicted too, with lists like: 'Three United players whose surname is a country'; 'Five United outfield players who have played in goal for the Reds'; 'The 10 oldest players to have played for the club.' Believe me – once you start you will not stop.

I know John White because I am honorary president of the United supporters' club he runs – Carryduff in Belfast. If John has worked on this book with just a tenth of the energy he devotes to that club, the Red cause and to charity, it will be more than an experience – and it will give you and me even more talking points to liven up conversations.

Yours in United

Eamonn Holmes

10 EVENTS IN JANUARY

1. 1 JANUARY 1974
George Best says farewell and Stewart Houston makes his debut
Queens Park Rangers 3   Manchester United 0
This game marked the end of George Best's association with Manchester United – an association which had lasted over 10 years. In Best's last ever game for the club, Tommy Docherty introduced Stewart Houston to the United defence. Houston went on to serve United loyally until his own departure to Sheffield United in July 1980.

2. 3 JANUARY 1905
United set a record successive League victory run
United win their fourteenth successive League game in Division 2 when they beat Bolton Wanderers 4-2 away (Allan 2, Peddie and Williams). It was an all-time League record that was later equalled by Bristol City and Preston North End. Disappointingly, United failed to gain promotion to the top flight, finishing the season in third place.

3. 5 JANUARY 1932
James W Gibson is appointed a Director
At a board meeting at Old Trafford, James W Gibson was elected as a director of the club. As with John H Davies before him, James Gibson proved to be the club's saviour when in December 1931 he placed £2,000 at the club's disposal (to pay the mortgage on Old Trafford and the monies owing to the Inland Revenue) and also ensured that the players received their wages.

4. 10 JANUARY 1948
Aston Villa 4   Manchester United 6
United beat Aston Villa 6-4 at Villa Park when the two sides met in the Third Round of the FA Cup. Villa were the first to score with a goal after only 13 seconds but then United hit back and at the interval were cruising to victory having scored five goals. In the second half Villa put up a tremendous fight in the mud and rain to trail 4-5 but Stan Pearson scored his second goal of the game to give United a 6-4 victory. The other United goalscorers were Morris (2), Delaney and Rowley. United were to go all the way to Wembley and win the FA Cup, defeating Blackpool 4-2 in the Final.

5. 11 JANUARY 1904
United's (then Newton Heath) longest FA Cup tie
Newton Heath played their most protracted FA Cup tie against Small Heath (later Birmingham City). After three replays and over seven hours of football, the Heathens triumphed 3-1 at Hyde Road. The Newton Heath goals were scored by Arkesden (2) and Grassam. The reward for wining the tie was a name in the hat for the First Round.

6. 17 JANUARY 1948
The highest ever Football League attendance record is set at Maine Road
Manchester United 1   Arsenal 1
This League game was played at Manchester City's Maine Road ground due to wartime bomb damage at Old Trafford. The crowd of 82,950 (although some records show a paying crowd of 81,962) is the record crowd for an English League game. Jack Rowley scored for United.

7. 18 JANUARY 1964
Law, Best and Charlton play their first game together
West Bromwich Albion 1   Manchester United 4
The first game in which Matt Busby played the trio of Law, Best and Charlton together in the same match. United, with the predatory instinct of Law, the class of Charlton and the genius of the young Irishman were simply too good for the home side who suffered a 4-1 defeat.
The goals, appropriately, were scored by Law (2), Best and Charlton.

8. 20 JANUARY 1994
The football world mourns the death of Sir Matt Busby
The football world was united in mourning the death of Sir Matt Busby, the father of Manchester United, aged 84. The City of Manchester had not witnessed such scenes of grief since the Munich air disaster in 1958.

9. 22 JANUARY 1910
United play their last game at Bank Street, Clayton
Manchester United 5
Tottenham Hotspur 0
This game was the last game played by United at their Bank Street ground before the opening of Old Trafford. The game should have been United's first match at their new home, but building work had not been completed on time. (Scorers: Roberts 2, Connor, Hooper and Meredith.)

10. 25 JANUARY 1995
Eric sees red at Selhurst Park
Eric Cantona was sent off at Selhurst Park in United's 2-2 Premiership draw with Crystal Palace. Dismissed after leaping on to the advertising hoarding and attacking a man in the crowd for hurling racial abuse at him, the incident was dubbed Eric's Kung Fu Attack by the media.

Eric Cantona

FACTS AND FIGURES

10 MANCHESTER UNITED FACTS

1. When they were formed in 1878 they were known as Newton Heath Lancashire & Yorkshire Railway. They became Manchester United in 1902.

2. They moved to Old Trafford, from Bank Street, Clayton, in 1910.

3. Between 1945 and 1949 they had to play their home games at Manchester City's Maine Road ground because Old Trafford suffered bomb damage during the war.

4. They are the only team to have won the FA Cup by defeating a First Division club in every Round (1990).

5. United hold the record for the most FA Cup wins with 9 (1909, 1948, 1963, 1977, 1983, 1985, 1990, 1994 and 1996).

6. They were the first English club to win the European Cup (4-1 versus Benfica at Wembley in 1968).

7. When United won the FA Carling Premier League in 1993 they had exactly the same record when they won the First Division Championship in 1965 (P 42 W 24 D 12 L 6).

8. In 1994 United became the first club to win the League Championship, FA Cup and FA Charity Shield in the same season.

9. In 1996 they became the first English club to win the domestic Double twice (FA Carling Premier League and FA Cup).

10. Manchester United became a limited company (Manchester United plc) in June 1991.

10 UNITED RECORDS

1. United's record defeat is 0-7 (Blackburn Rovers (a) 10.04.26 Div. 1, Aston Villa (a) 27.12.30 Div. 1 and Wolverhampton Wanderers (a) 26.12.31 Div. 2).

2. United's record score in European competition is their 10-0 win over RSC Anderlecht at Maine Road in a European Cup Preliminary Round on 26.09.56 (the aggregate score of 12-0 is also a record).

3. The club record receipts are £739,841 for their UEFA Champions League Semi-Final, 2nd Leg game against Borussia Dortmund on 23.04.97.

4. United's record transfer fee paid is £12.6 million to Aston Villa for Dwight Yorke in August 1998.

5. United's record transfer fee received is £7million paid by Inter Milan for Paul Ince in July 1995.

6. The record number of international caps won by a Manchester United player is 106 won by Bobby Charlton for England (first v Scotland on 19.04.58 and last v West Germany on 14.06.70).

7. United's record goalscorer in a single season is Denis Law who scored 46 goals in season 1963-64 (30 League, 10 FA Cup and 6 European Cup-Winners' Cup).

8. The record number of wins by United in a single season is 41 during the 1993-94 season (27 League, 6 FA Cup, 6 League Cup and 2 European Cup).

9. United's record league home win is their 10-1 Division 1 victory over Wolverhampton Wanderers at North Road, Monsall on 15.10.1892. (United were known as Newton Heath at the time.)

10. United's record start to a season is 13 victories and 2 draws in their opening 15 games of the 1985-86 season.

10 OLD TRAFFORD FACTS

1. It was designed by Archibald Leitch.

2. The first game to be played in Old Trafford was Manchester United versus Liverpool on 19 February 1910 (Liverpool won 4-3).

3. It staged the 1911 FA Cup Replay between Newcastle United and Bradford City.

4. United's record League attendance at Old Trafford is 70,504 for their game with Aston Villa on 27 December 1920.

5. On 11 March 1941 Old Trafford was virtually demolished following a German bombing raid on Manchester. The damage was so severe United had to play their home games at Maine Road from 1945 to 1949.

6. The first ever League Cup Semi-Final Replay was played at Old Trafford in 1961 (Aston Villa v Burnley).

7. During the 1966 World Cup Finals in England Old Trafford staged three Group games.

8. Chelsea beat Leeds United at Old Trafford in the 1970 FA Cup Final Replay.

9. United's best ever League win at Old Trafford was their 9-0 demolition of Ipswich Town on 4 March 1995.

10. Old Trafford staged several Group games when the European Championships were played in England in 1996.

MANCHESTER UNITED'S RECORD ATTENDANCES

FA Cup at Bank Street, Clayton	35,500 for the 3rd Round game versus Aston Villa on 24 February 1906
FA Cup at Old Trafford	66,350 for the 5th Round game versus Sheffield Wednesday on 20 February 1960
Football League at Bank Street, Clayton	40,000 for the game versus Bristol City on 5 September 1903
Football League at Old Trafford	70,504 for the game versus Aston Villa on 27 December 1920
Football League at Maine Road	82,950 for the game versus Arsenal on 17 January 1948
Football League Cup	63,418 for the game versus Manchester City on 17 December 1969

NEWTON HEATH AND MANCHESTER UNITED'S GROUNDS

1. 1880-93   North Road, Newton Heath
2. 1893-1910   Bank Street, Clayton
3. 1910-Present Old Trafford

10 GROUNDS IN ENGLAND WHERE MANCHESTER UNITED HAVE PLAYED A HOME GAME

1. North Road, Monsall   Home 1878-1893
2. Bank Street, Clayton   Home 1893-1910
3. Old Trafford   Home 1910-
4. Maine Road   Manchester City
5. Goodison Park   Everton
6. Leeds Road   Huddersfield Town
7. Villa Park   Aston Villa
8. Anfield   Liverpool
9. Victoria Ground   Stoke City
10. Home Park   Plymouth Argyle

Nos 4 – 7: After World War II United had to play their home League and Cup games at Maine Road because Old Trafford had been bombed during the War. However, when Manchester City were at home United had to borrow another ground.

Nos 8 and 9: At the start of the 1971-72 season United were ordered by the Football Association to play their first two home games away from Old Trafford because of a knife throwing incident towards the end of season 1970-71.

No. 10: United were ordered by UEFA to play their home First Round, Second Leg ECWC game versus AS Saint-Etienne away from Old Trafford as a result of crowd trouble in France during the First Leg.

10 CHARITY SHIELD WINS FOR UNITED

1. 1908 Replay v Queens Park Rangers   4-0
2. 1911   v Swindon Town   8-4
3. 1952   v Newcastle United   4-2
4. 1956   v Manchester City   1-0
5. 1957   v Aston Villa   4-0
6. 1983   v Liverpool   2-0
7. 1993   v Arsenal   1-1 (5-4 on pens)
8. 1994   v Blackburn Rovers   2-0
9. 1996   v Newcastle United   4-0
10. 1997   v Chelsea   1-1 (4-2 pens)

FESTIVE FIXTURES

40 OCCASIONS WHEN MANCHESTER UNITED PLAYED A GAME ON NEW YEARS DAY

1. 1907 beat Aston Villa 1-0 (h) Division 1
2. 1908 beat Bury (a) Division 1
3. 1909 beat Notts County 4-3 (h) Division 1
4. 1910 beat Bradford City 2-0 (a) Division 1
5. 1912 beat Woolwich Arsenal 2-0 (h) Division 1
6. 1913 beat Bradford City 2-0 (h) Division 1
7. 1914 beat West Bromwich Albion 1-0 (h) Division 1
8. 1915 lost 1-2 to Bradford City (h) Division 1
9. 1920 drew 0-0 with Liverpool (a) Division 1
10. 1921 lost 3-6 to Newcastle United (a) Division 1
11. 1923 beat Barnsley 1-0 (h) Division 2
12. 1925 beat Chelsea 1-0 (h) Division 2
13. 1927 beat Sheffield United 5-0 (h) Division 1
14. 1929 drew 2-2 with Aston Villa (h) Division 1
15. 1931 drew 0-0 with Leeds United (h) Division 1
16. 1935 beat Southampton 3-0 (h) Division 2
17. 1936 beat Barnsley 3-0 (a) Division 2
18. 1937 beat Sunderland 2-1 (h) Division 1
19. 1938 drew 2-2 with Newcastle United (a) Division 2
20. 1948 beat Burnley 5-0 (h) Division 1
21. 1949 beat Arsenal 2-0 (h) Division 1
22. 1953 beat Derby County 1-0 (h) Division 1
23. 1955 beat Blackpool 4-1 (h) Division 1
24. 1957 beat Chelsea 3-0 (h) Division 1
25. 1966 lost 1-2 to Liverpool (a) Division 1
26. 1972 lost 0-3 to West Ham United (a) Division 1
27. 1974 lost 0-3 to Queens Park Rangers (a) division 1
28. 1977 beat Aston Villa 2-0 (h) Division 1
29. 1983 beat Aston Villa 3-1 (h) Division 1
30. 1985 lost 1-2 to Sheffield Wednesday (h) Division 1
31. 1986 beat Birmingham City 1-0 (h) Division 1
32. 1987 beat Newcastle United 4-1 (h) Division 1
33. 1988 drew 0-0 with Charlton Athletic (h) Division 1
34. 1989 beat Liverpool 3-1 (h) Division 1

35. 1990 drew 0-0 with Queens Park Rangers (h) Division 1
36. 1991 beat Tottenham Hotspur 2-1 (a) Division 1
37. 1992 lost 1-4 to Queens Park Rangers (h) Division 1
38. 1994 drew 0-0 with Leeds United (h) Premier League
39. 1996 lost 1-4 to Tottenham Hotspur (a) Premier League
40. 1997 0-0 with Aston Villa (h) Premier League

2 OCCASIONS WHEN NEWTON HEATH PLAYED A GAME ON CHRISTMAS DAY

1. 1896 beat Manchester City 2-1 (h) Division 2
2. 1897 beat Manchester City 1-0 (a) Division 2

7 OCCASIONS WHEN NEWTON HEATH PLAYED A GAME ON NEW YEARS DAY

1. 1892 drew 1-1 with Nottingham Forest (h) Football Aliance
2. 1895 beat Burslem Port Vale 3-0 (h) Division 2
3. 1896 beat Grimsby Town 3-2 (h) Division 2
4. 1897 lost 0-2 to Newcastle United (a) Division 2
5. 1898 beat Burton Swifts 4-0 (h) Division 2
6. 1901 beat Middlesbrough 2-1 (a) Division 2
7. 1902 lost 0-2 to Preston North End (h) Division 2

31 OCCASIONS WHEN MANCHESTER UNITED PLAYED A GAME ON CHRISTMAS DAY

1. 1902 drew 1-1 with Manchester City (h) Division 2
2. 1903 beat Chesterfield 3-1 (h) Division 2
3. 1905 drew 0-0 with Chelsea (h) Division 2
4. 1906 drew 0-0 with Liverpool (h) Division 1
5. 1907 beat Bury 2-1 (h)
6. 1908 lost 1-2 Newcastle United (a) Division 1
7. 1909 lost 0-3 to Sheffield Wednesday (h) Division 1
8. 1911 lost 0-1 to Bradford City (h) Division 1
9. 1912 beat Chelsea 4-1 (a) Division 1
10. 1913 lost 0-1 to Everton (h) Division 1
11. 1920 beat Aston Villa 4-3 (a) Division 1
12. 1922 lost 1-2 to West Ham United (h) Division 2

13. 1923 lost 1-2 to Barnsley (h) Division 2

14. 1924 1-1 with Middlesbrough (a) Division 2

15. 1925 beat Bolton Wanderers 2-1 (h) Division 1

16. drew 1-1 with Tottenham Hotspur (a) Division 1

17. 1928 drew 1-1 with Sheffield United (h) Division 1

18. 1929 drew 0-0 with Birmingham City (h) Division 1

19. 1930 lost 1-3 to Bolton Wanderers (a) Division 1

20. 1931 beat Wolves 3-2 (h) Division 2

21. 1933 lost 1-2 to Grimsby Town (h) Division 2

22. 1934 beat Notts County 2-1 (h) Division 2

23. 1936 beat Bolton Wanderers 1-0 (h) Division 1

24. 1946 drew 2-2 with Bolton Wanderers (a) Division 1

25. 1947 beat Portsmouth 3-2 (h) Division 1

26. 1948 drew 0-0 with Liverpool (h) Division 1

27. 1950 lost 1-2 to Sunderland (a) Division 1

28. 1951 beat Fulham 3-2 (h) Division 1

29. 1952 drew 0-0 with Blackpool (a) Division 1

30. 1953 beat Sheffield Wednesday 5-2 Division 1

31. 1957 beat Luton Town 3-0 (h) Division 1

MANCHESTER UNITED'S RECORD SCORES

Pre-war in the Football League — Newton Heath 10 Wolverhampton Wanderers 1 on 15 October 1892.
(Newton Heath beat Walsall Town Swifts 14-0 on 9 March 1895 but the game was declared void because of the state of the pitch at Bank Street, Clayton.)

Post-war in the Football League — Manchester United 8 Queens Park Rangers 1 on 19 March 1969.

FA Carling Premier League — Manchester United 9 Ipswich Town 0 on 4 March 1995.

Pre-war in the FA Cup — Newton Heath 7 West Manchester 0 on 12 December 1896.
Manchester United 7 Accrington Stanley 0 on 1 November 1902.
Manchester United 7 Staple Hill 0 on 13 January 1906.

Post-war in the FA Cup — Manchester United 8 Yeovil Town 0 on 12 February 1949.

Football League Cup — Manchester United 7 Newcastle United 2 on 27 October 1976.

FA Charity Shield — Manchester United 8 Swindon Town 4 on 25 September 1911.

European Cup — Manchester United 10 RSC Anderlecht 0 on 26 September 1956.
(This game was played at Maine Road.)

European Cup-Winners' Cup — Manchester United 6 Willem II 0 on 15 October 1963.

Inter-Cities Fairs Cup/UEFA Cup — Manchester United 6 Djurgadens IF 1 on 27 September 1964.

MANCHESTER UNITED'S WORST 3 DEFEATS

1.	0-7 v Bristol Rovers (a)	Division 1	10.04.26
2.	0-7 v Aston Villa (a)	Division 1	27.12.30
3.	0-7 v Wolves (a)	Division 2	26.12.31

3 GAMES AT OLD TRAFFORD IN CONSECUTIVE DAYS

1.	United 4 Portsmouth 1	English League Division 1	07.05.88
2.	United v Manchester City	Arthur Albiston Testimonial	08.05.88
3.	United 2 Wimbledon 1	English League Division 1	09.05.88

NEWTON HEATH AND MANCHESTER UNITED'S CLUB COLOURS

1.	1892-1894	Red & White Quartered Jerseys, White Shorts
2.	1894-1896	Green & Gold Jerseys, White Shorts
2.	1896-1902	White Jerseys, Blue Shorts
3.	1902-1923	Red Jerseys, White Shorts
4.	1923-1927	White Jerseys (with a Red V), White Shorts
5.	1927-1934	Red Jerseys, White Shorts
6.	1934	Cherry & White Hooped Jerseys, White Shorts
7.	1934-Present	Red Jerseys, White Shorts

3 CUP COMPETITIONS WON BY MANCHESTER UNITED WHEN PLAYING IN A BLUE KIT

1.	1948 FA Cup Final	Manchester United 4 Blackpool 2
2.	1968 European Cup Final	Manchester United 4 Benfica 1 (aet)
3.	1992 Rumbelows League Cup Final	Manchester United 1 Nottingham Forest 0

5 OCCASIONS WHEN MANCHESTER UNITED WORE THEIR GREY STRIP IN A COMPETITIVE GAME

1.	v Aston Villa (a)	lost 3-1	19.08.95
2.	v Arsenal (a)	lost 1-0	04.11.95
3.	v Nottingham Forest (a)	drew 1-1	27.11.95
4.	v Liverpool (a)	lost 2-0	17.12.95
5.	v Southampton (a)	lost 3-1	13.04.96

All games were played in the FA Carling Premier League

THE ONLY 3 PLAYERS TO SCORE FOR MANCHESTER UNITED IN A COMPETITIVE GAME WEARING THE GREY KIT

1. David Beckham   v Aston Villa (a)
2. Eric Cantona (pen)   v Nottingham Forest (a)
3. Ryan Giggs   v Southampton (a)

3 SPORTSWEAR COMPANIES THAT HAVE MANUFACTURED MANCHESTER UNITED'S KIT

1. Admiral
2. Adidas
3. Umbro

2 COMPANIES WHICH HAVE SPONSORED MANCHESTER UNITED'S FAMILY STAND

1. Panini Stickers
2. McDonalds

THE 8 MANCHESTER UNITED PLAYERS WHO LOST THEIR LIVES IN THE MUNICH AIR DISASTER

1. Geoffrey Bent
2. Roger Byrne
3. Eddie Colman
4. Duncan Edwards
5. Mark Jones
6. David Pegg
7. Tommy Taylor
8. Liam Whelan

Matt Busby leads out the Busby Babes to face Aston Villa in the 1957 FA Cup Final

9 MANCHESTER UNITED MANAGERS/PLAYERS WHO HAVE RECEIVED HONOURS FROM THE QUEEN

1. Sir Matt Busby CBE
2. Sir Bobby Charlton CBE
3. Alex Ferguson CBE
4. Mark Hughes MBE
5. Sammy McIlroy MBE
6. Bryan Robson OBE
7. Gordon Strachan OBE
8. Ray Wilkins MBE
9. Sir Walter Winterbottom CBE

Ray Wilkins

8 PAST OR PRESENT MANCHESTER UNITED PLAYERS WHO HAVE APPEARED IN A TELEVISION ADVERTISEMENT

1. George Best: Cookstown sausages
2. Peter Schmeichel: Reebok boots (he played a pig farmer) and Danish bacon
3. Ryan Giggs: Reebok boots (he played a flower seller)
4. Ray Wilkins: Tango fizzy orange drink (his voice was used)
5. Eric Cantona: Eurostar and Nike boots
6. David Beckham: Brylcreem and Adidas boots
7. Andy Cole: Reebok boots (he played a fish and chip shop worker)
8. Paul Ince: Adidas boots

10 MANCHESTER UNITED PLAYERS AND MAKES OF FOOTBALL BOOTS THEY WORE OR HAD CONTRACTS WITH

1. George Best   Stylo
2. Ian Storey-Moore   Hummel
3. Lou Macari   Admiral
4. Bryan Robson   New Balance
5. Brian McClair   Puma
6. Eric Cantona   Nike
7. Ryan Giggs   Reebok
8. Roy Keane   Diadora
9. David Beckham   Adidas
10. Dwight Yorke   Mizuno

David Beckham

12 CELEBRITIES WHO SUPPORT MANCHESTER UNITED

1. Eamonn Holmes
2. Mick Hucknall
3. Zoe Ball
4. Angus Deayton
5. Shane Ritchie
6. Terry Christian
7. John Virgo
8. Ulrika Jonsson
9. Ian McShane
10. Gary Rhodes
11. Jimmy Cricket
12. Wasim Akram

20 NICKNAMES OF MANCHESTER UNITED PLAYERS

1.	Gunner	Jack Rowley
2.	Happy	Nobby Stiles
3.	The King	Denis Law
4.	El Beatle	George Best
5.	Merlin	Gordon Hill
6.	The Black Pearl of Inchicore	Paul McGrath
7.	The Black Prince	Alex Dawson
8.	The Judge	Lou Macari
9.	Sparky	Mark Hughes
10.	Chips	Arthur Albiston
11.	Bamber	Alan Gowling
12.	Pancho	Stuart Pearson
13.	Baby Faced Assassin	Ole Gunnar Solskjaer
14.	Cowboy	Bill Foulkes
15.	Robbo	Bryan Robson
16.	Choccy	Brian McClair
17.	Knocker	Enoch West
18.	Snake Hips	Eddie Colman
19.	Butch	Ray Wilkins
20.	Stroller	George Graham

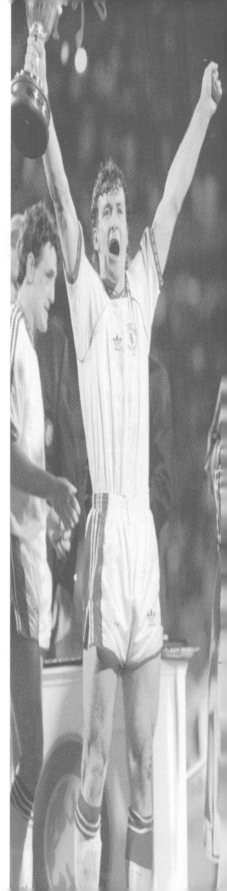

10 SONGS SUNG BY THE MANCHESTER UNITED TEAM

1. We Will Stand Together
2. United, Manchester United
3. Look Around
4. Yellow Submarine
5. Congratulations
6. Storm In A Teacup
7. Raindrops Keep Falling On My Head
8. Precious Memories
9. We're Gonna Do It Again
10. Move Move Move (The Red Tribe)

10 SONGS ABOUT MANCHESTER UNITED OR MANCHESTER UNITED PLAYERS

1. United United
2. Red Devils
3. Willie Morgan On The Wing
4. The Manchester United Calypso
5. Rah Rah Man United
6. Glory Glory Man United
7. Belfast Boy
8. Denis The Menace
9. Ryan Giggs We Love You
10. Eric The King

10 CHANTS FROM THE TERRACES OF OLD TRAFFORD

1. Come On You Reds
2. U – Ni – Ted (repeated several times)
3. Alex Ferguson's Red and White Army (repeated several times)
4. Ooh Aah Eric Cantona (repeated several times)
5. Stand Up If You Love Man U (repeated several times)
6. There's Only One UNITED (repeated several times)
7. Fergie, Fergie, Give Us A Wave, Fergie Give Us A Wave
8. Boom Boom Boom Let Me Hear You Say Keano, KEANO
9. You Only Came To See UNITED, Came To See UNITED (repeated)
10. Andy Cole, Andy Cole, Andy Andy Cole. He Gets The Ball, He Scores A Goal, Andy Andy Cole

70 ITEMS AVAILABLE IN THE MANCHESTER UNITED MEGASTORE AT OLD TRAFFORD

1. Football shirts, shorts and socks
2. Jackets
3. Tracksuits
4. T-Shirts
5. Wallet
6. Shoe Bag
7. Water Bottle
8. Holdall
9. Shin Guards
10. Goalkeeper's gloves
11. Football
12. Sweat Top
13. Pique Top
14. Warm Up T-Shirt
15. Fleece Jacket
16. Crew Neck T-Shirt
17. Zip Neck Polo Shirt
18. V-Neck Sweatshirt
19. Popper Pants
20. Duvet Cover
21. Curtains
22. Wallpaper and Border
23. Pyjamas
24. Towelling Dressing Gown
25. Slippers
26. Towel
27. Door Plaque
28. Lampshade and Base
29. Bean Bag
30. Hats
31. Baseball Caps
32. Scarves
33. Pencil Case Set
34. A4 Ring Binder
35. Flip Photograph Album
36. A4 Spiral Bound Pad
37. Hard Backed Address Book
38. Pencil Tin
39. Organiser
40. Pens
41. Art Pack
42. Autograph Book and Pen
43. Wall Clock
44. Alarm Clock
45. 3-D Alarm Clock
46. Watches
47. Stereo CD/Radio/Cassette Recorder
48. 2-in-1 Personal Stereo
49. Replica Stadium
50. Teddy Bear
51. Bubble Bath
52. Body Wash
53. Back Pack
54. Boot Bag
55. Wristbands
56. Mugs
57. Half Pint Glass
58. Pint Glass
59. Conical Glass
60. Football Shape Mug
61. Pint Tankard
62. Ties
63. Keyrings
64. Framed Prints
65. Player Postcards
66. Video Cassette Tapes
67. Books
68. Bike Helmet
69. Y-Frame Bike
70. BMX Bike

US CONNECTION

10 NORTH AMERICAN SOCCER LEAGUE TEAMS MANCHESTER UNITED PLAYERS HAVE PLAYED FOR

1. Portland Timbers
2. Tampa Bay Rowdies
3. Vancouver Whitecaps
4. Los Angeles Aztecs
5. Fort Lauderdale Strikers
6. San Jose Earthquakes
7. Detroit Express
8. New England Tea Men
9. Jacksonville Tea Men
10. Tulsa Roughnecks

10 MORE NORTH AMERICAN SOCCER LEAGUE TEAMS MANCHESTER UNITED PLAYERS HAVE PLAYED FOR

1. Seattle Sounders
2. Chicago Sting
3. California Surf
4. Toronto Blizzard
5. Montreal Manic
6. New York Arrows
7. Kansas Comets
8. Tacoma Stars
9. Miami Toros
10. Atlanta Chief

IRISH CONNECTION

10 IRISH TEAMS MANCHESTER UNITED PLAYERS HAVE PLAYED FOR

1. Ballymena United
2. Bohemians
3. Cliftonville
4. Coleraine
5. Cork
6. Derry City
7. Glenavon
8. Glentoran
9. Shamrock Rovers
10. Shelbourne

SCOTTISH CONNECTION

10 SCOTTISH CLUBS MANCHESTER UNITED PLAYERS HAVE PLAYED FOR

1. Aberdeen
2. Airdrieonians
3. Dundee
4. Dundee United
5. Glasgow Celtic
6. Glasgow Rangers
7. Heart of Midlothian
8. Motherwell
9. St Johnstone
10. St Mirren

10 OFFICIAL MANCHESTER UNITED SUPPORTERS CLUBS BASED IN ENGLAND

1. Asbourne
2. Barnsley
3. Black Country
4. Carlisle & District
5. Cleveland
6. Dukinfield & Hyde
7. Glossop
8. Macclesfield
9. Plymouth
10. Stalybridge

10 OFFICIAL MANCHESTER UNITED SUPPORTERS CLUBS BASED IN NORTHERN IRELAND

1. Carryduff
2. Castledawson
3. Coleraine
4. Foyle
5. Glenowen
6. Newtownards
7. Portavogie
8. Portrush
9. Strabane
10. Warrenpoint

10 OFFICIAL MANCHESTER UNITED SUPPORTERS CLUBS BASED IN WALES

1. Abergele and Coast
2. Aberystwyth and District
3. Central Powys
4. Chester and North Wales
5. Colwyn Bay and District
6. Glamorgan and Gwent
7. Gwynedd
8. North Powys
9. Pontyprydd
10. Swansea

10 OFFICIAL MANCHESTER UNITED SUPPORTERS CLUBS BASED OUTSIDE THE BRITISH ISLES

1. Belgium
2. Canada
3. German Friends
4. Holland
5. Luxembourg
6. Malta
7. New Zealand
8. Swiss Devils
9. Tokyo
10. Western Australia

10 OFFICIAL MANCHESTER UNITED SUPPORTERS CLUBS BASED IN THE REPUBLIC OF IRELAND

1. Arklow
2. Bundoran
3. Carlow
4. Clara
5. Cork Area
6. Dundalk
7. Kildare
8. Kilkenny
9. Limerick
10. Sligo

10 MORE OFFICIAL MANCHESTER UNITED SUPPORTERS CLUBS BASED OUTSIDE THE BRITISH ISLES

2. German Reds
3. Gibraltar
4. Iceland
5. Malaysia
6. Mauritius
7. Scandanavia
8. South Africa
9. South Australia
10. USA

United's fanatical Red Army.

10 EVENTS IN FEBRUARY

1.   1 FEBRUARY 1958
Busby Babes' last game on English soil
Arsenal 4   Manchester United 5

The Busby Babes played their last game on English soil as United beat Arsenal, at the Arsenal Stadium, in their League encounter. United were chasing their third consecutive First Division Championship and led the home side 3-0 at half-time with goals from Duncan Edwards, Tommy Taylor and Bobby Charlton. In the second half Arsenal scored three times in under three minutes (the first Arsenal goal was scored by David Herd, who later became a United player) taking the score, suddenly to 3-3. The home side's fightback did no more than lift United's game and the Reds scored twice more through Dennis Viollet and a second from Tommy Taylor. Arsenal pulled a late goal back but it wasn't enough.

The United line-up was from: Gregg, Foulkes, Byrne, Colman, Jones, Edwards, Morgan, Charlton, Taylor, Viollet, Scanlon.

2.   1 FEBRUARY 1961
United suffer their worst home post war defeat
Manchester United 2   Sheffield Wednesday 7

United were humbled at home in the FA Cup. In their Fourth Round Replay with Sheffield Wednesday, the Yorkshire side won 7-2. Dawson and Pearson scored for United. Only four days earlier United had held Sheffield Wednesday to a 0-0 draw at Hillsborough.

3.   5 FEBRUARY 1958
The Last Line-up
Red Star Belgrade 3   Manchester United 3

Manchester United were in Belgrade for their European Cup Quarter-Final, Second Leg game with the Yugoslavian Champions. United had won the Home Leg 2-1 a fortnight earlier and were poised to reach their second successive semi-final in the competition. The Busby Babes quietened the intimidating 55,000 home fans with their breathtaking football and were soon 3-0 up on the night, and 5-1 ahead on aggregate. The fiercely partisan home crowd then turned on the Babes which seemed to unnerve the Austrian referee, Karl Kainer. A number of match reports that followed the game, notably that of Henry Rose of the *Daily Express*, questioned a number of the referee's decisions. Two minutes after the interval Red Star Belgrade scored through Kostic and were then awarded a penalty after Foulkes and Tasic tangled in the box, only for Foulkes to fall on top of Tasic as he lay on the grass. Foulkes maintained that Tasic lost his balance and as he was falling brought Foulkes down on top of him. However, the penalty decision stood and was converted by Tasic. Red Star's second goal of the game sent the crowd into a frenzy and although they scored again with minutes remaining, United were through 5-4 on aggregate. United's assistant manager, Jimmy Murphy, missed the trip to Belgrade as he was in Cardiff managing the Welsh national side which defeated Israel 2-1 in a World Cup qualifying game.

4.   6 FEBRUARY 1958
The Munich Air Disaster

The day after their 3-3 draw with Red Star Belgrade the United team, together with club officials and journalists, left Belgrade for Manchester, with a brief scheduled stop-off at Munich Airport en-route. At approximately 2.00 p.m. the twin-engined Elizabethan jet, named Lord Burleigh, was ready for take-off with Captain Kenneth Rayment, second in command at the controls. Captain James Thain had flown the plane out to Belgrade but handed over to Captain Rayment for the flight home.

At 2.31 p.m. the aircraft control tower were informed that 609 Zulu Uniform was rolling. As the plane rolled down the runway Captain Thain noticed the port pressure gauge fluctuating shortly after full power had been engaged and the engine sounded strange during acceleration. Captain Rayment abandoned take-off within 40 seconds of the start. The problem was termed a 'boost surge' whereby the engines over-accelerated because of the very rich mixture of fuel. Apparently this was a common problem with the Elizabethan. At 2.34 p.m. 609 Zulu Uniform was given permission to attempt a second take-off by air traffic control but once again the plane came to a halt. After the second aborted attempt to take-off the passengers returned to the airport lounge.

It had started to snow heavily and many of the players were of the opinion that they would not be flying home that afternoon. Duncan Edwards sent a telegram to his landlady back home in Manchester which read: 'All flights cancelled, flying tomorrow. Duncan.' After a fifteen-minute delay everyone boarded the plane again. A number of the passengers, notably Duncan Edwards, Mark Jones, Tommy Taylor, Eddie Colman and Frank Swift, decided to move to the rear of the plane where they believed it to be a safer place to sit. Following discussions between Captain Thain, Captain Rayment and William Black (the Airport engineer), 609 Zulu Uniform was on the move again. Problems ensued once more as the plane sped down the runway. The air speed indicator at first read 117 knots and then dropped to 105 knots. The jet shot off the runway and went straight through a fence, then across a road before its port wing struck a nearby house. Part of the jet's tail and it's wing were instantly ripped off and the house caught fire. The cockpit hit a tree, the starboard side of the fuselage hit a wooden hut which contained a truck loaded with fuel and tyres. The truck exploded upon impact.

Bill Foulkes speaking after the crash, recalled hearing a bang, then after a few minutes of unconsciousness, remembered seeing a hole in the plane directly in front of him. Foulkes and United keeper, Harry Gregg, performed heroics as they helped team mates and passengers from the smouldering wreckage time after time. The injured, including a seriously hurt Matt Busby, were taken to the nearby Rechts de Isar Hospital. However, it was not until the next day that the world became aware of the true horror of the crash. Duncan Edwards' telegram was delivered at approximately 5.00 p.m., less than two hours after the crash.

Matt Busby lay in an oxygen tent, Bobby Charlton had a bandage wrapped around his head, Jackie Blanchflower had a badly gashed arm, Ray Wood suffered a cut face and concussion, Albert Scanlon's skull was fractured. Duncan Edwards had serious injuries, Dennis Viollet had a gashed head together with injuries to his face whilst both Ken Morgans and Johnny Berry lay motionless in bed. Close by the United players lay the journalist, Frank Taylor.

The Busby Babes killed instantly in the crash were: Geoff Bent, Roger Byrne, Eddie Colman, Mark Jones, David Pegg, Tommy Taylor and Liam Whelan. Walter Crickmere, the Club Secretary, first team trainer Tom Curry and coach, Bert Whalley all perished too. Eight of the nine journalists on the flight (Alf Clarke, Don Davies, George Follows, Tom Jackson, Archie Ledbrooke, Henry Rose, Frank Swift and Eric Thompson) also died, as did one of the aircrew, the travel agent who arranged the trip, a supporter and two other passengers. In all, twenty-three people died in the crash (Duncan Edwards and Captain Rayment died in hospital from their injuries) and sixteen people survived. Two of the United players who survived the crash, Jackie Blanchflower and Johnny Berry, never played competitive football again. The Munich air disaster was undoubtedly one of football's blackest days.

5.   7 FEBRUARY 1970
Best Magic
Northampton Town 2   Manchester United 8

George Best returned from suspension and was in the United line-up that faced Northampton Town away in the FA Cup, Fifth Round. Best was unstoppable as he carved through the home defence time after time, scoring two hat-tricks in the process. United won 8-2 with Brian Kidd helping himself to United's other two goals.

6.   13 FEBRUARY 1994
Record breaking unbeaten home run is set

United set a club record of thirty-six games unbeaten at home in all competitions when they beat Sheffield Wednesday 1-0 (scorer: Ryan Giggs), in the First Leg of the Semi-Final of the Coca-Cola Cup. The run began on 21 November 1992 with a 3-0 league win over Oldham Athletic.

7.   15 FEBRUARY 1945
Matt Busby takes charge at Old Trafford

Matt Busby was born in Bellshill, Lanarkshire in 1909. His father was a miner, who died on the Somme in World War I. The young Busby followed his father's footsteps down the pit but he always had a dream that one day he would earn his living as a footballer. In 1928 that dream became a reality when he joined Manchester City. An outstanding right-half for Manchester City, he won an FA Cup Winners' medal with them in 1934 and then moved on to Liverpool in 1936. He captained Scotland and the British Services' team during the Second World War.

Taking up his appointment at United he inherited an old team, whilst Old Trafford was a pile of rubble. However, ably assisted by his right-hand man, Jimmy Murphy, Matt Busby began the re-building process. He is enshrined forever within the history of Manchester United Football Club for building three great teams at Old Trafford the first of which he built around Johnny Carey. They were First

Sir Matt Busby

Division Runners-up in 1947, 1948 and 1949 and winners of the FA Cup in 1948. Busby's style of management was a breath of fresh air - unlike his predecessors he joined his players on the training field, a concept unheard of at the time. Matt Busby put all his faith and trust in youth. During the 1950s United won the First Division Championship 3 times (1952, 1956 and 1957), were Runners-up twice (1951 and 1959), FA Cup finalists in 1957 and 1958, FA Charity Shield winners 3 times (1952, 1956 and 1957) and United's Youth Team won the first five FA Youth Cups (1953-1957).

After a tragedy like the Munich air disaster most ordinary men would have given up on football. In memory of the talent lost on that day he commenced the almost impossible task of re-building the team. Matt Busby built his third great side during the 1960s - a team containing United legends such as Law, Best and Charlton. The team of the 1960s thrilled fans up and down the country with their swashbuckling style, instilled in them by Matt Busby. Matt's philosophy to his players was simply for them to go on to the field and enjoy themselves. In the 1960s United won the FA Cup in 1963, were First Division Champions in 1965 and 1967, First Division Runners-up in 1964 and 1968, joint-holders of the FA Charity Shield in 1965 and 1967 and winners of the FA Youth Cup for the sixth time under his leadership in 1964. But the greatest night in Matt Busby's football life came at Wembley in May 1968. United, the pioneers of English football in European club competitions when Matt Busby defied FA orders and entered United in the 1956-57 European Cup, became the first English side to win the European Cup. That hot May evening, Busby's third great side beat Benfica of Portugal 4-1 after extra time.

In 1968 Matt Busby was named Manager of the Year, awarded the freedom of Manchester and given a knighthood by the Queen. Matt Busby was a man of the people, honest and hard working, respected by everyone and loved by the fans of his beloved Manchester United

8.   17 FEBRUARY 1910
Gales destroy United's Bank Street ground
Two days before the official opening of United's new home, Old Trafford, fierce gales struck the Manchester area. The old wooden stand at Bank Street was ripped apart by the gales as wreckage from it blew across the roadway, damaging a number of houses close by. Mercifully it wasn't a match day and no-one was injured.

9.   19 FEBRUARY 1910
Old Trafford is opened
Manchester United 3   Liverpool 4
United's move from Bank Street to Old Trafford took place midway through the 1909-10 season, and the very first game at Old Trafford was a fixture with Liverpool. A week before the game, invitations were sent out to local dignitaries. When completed, the ground was supposed to accommodate 100,000 spectators, but for this, the first game, a crowd of 45,000 turned up. Although United had several injury problems they raced to a 3-1 lead with goals from Homer, Sandy Turnbull and Wall. The Merseysiders fought back to level the game at 3-3 before grabbing a winner to spoil United's big day.

10.   21 FEBRUARY 1958
Duncan Edwards loses his brave battle for life
Fifteen days after suffering horrific injuries in the Munich air disaster, Duncan Edwards lost his brave battle for life. Duncan became the eighth Manchester United player to die as a result of the crash when his circulation failed as his kidney condition deteriorated. Manchester United, England and the football world lost the skills of a truly wonderful and gifted footballer. A stained-glass window serves as a permanent memorial to him in the Church of St Francis in the Priory, Dudley, Worcestershire.

THE PLAYERS

3 PLAYERS WHO PLAYED ONLY ONE GAME FOR NEWTON HEATH/MANCHESTER UNITED AND WHO SCORED IN THE GAME

1.	R. Stephenson	v Rotherham Town (h)	11.01.1896
2.	Bill Bainbridge	v Accrington Stanley (h)	09.01.46
3.	Albert Kinsey	v Chester City (h)	09.01.65

1 PLAYER WHO CAPTAINED BOTH NEWTON HEATH AND MANCHESTER UNITED

1.	Harry Stafford	1896-1902	Newton Heath
		1902-1903	Manchester United

8 POST-WAR MANCHESTER UNITED PLAYERS WHO PLAYED FOR THE CLUB PAST THEIR 35th BIRTHDAY

1.	Jack Warner	v Newcastle United (a)	22.04.50	38y 213d
2.	Bill Foulkes	v Southampton (h)	16.08.69	37y 222d
3.	Bryan Robson	v Coventry City (h)	08.05.94	37y 117d
4.	Les Sealey	v Aston Villa (n)	27.03.94	36y 179d
5.	Allenby Chilton	v Wolves (h)	23.02.55	36y 160d
6.	Jimmy Delaney	v Chelsea (a)	11.11.50	36y 69d
7.	Bobby Charlton	v Chelsea (a)	28.04.73	35y 198d
8.	Steve Bruce	v Leeds United (h)	17.04.96	35y 108d

No. 4 was the 1994 Coca-Cola Cup Final at Wembley

10 PLAYERS WHO PLAYED FOR BOTH NEWTON HEATH AND MANCHESTER UNITED

(Newton Heath became Manchester United in 1902)

1.	Walter Cartwright	1895-1904
2.	William Morgan	1896-1903
3.	Harry Stafford	1896-1903
4.	William Griffiths	1898-1905
5.	Hubert Lappin	1900-1903
6.	Alfred Schofield	1900-1907
7.	James Whitehouse	1900-1903
8.	John Banks	1901-1903
9.	Stephen Preston	1901-1903
10.	James Saunders	1901-1903

10 PLAYERS WHO PLAYED FOR NEWTON HEATH IN BOTH THE 19TH AND 20TH CENTURIES

1. Frank Barrett
2. Harry Stafford
3. Fred Erentz
4. William Morgan
5. Walter Cartwright
6. William Bryant
7. William Jackson
8. Joseph Cassidy
9. Alfred Ambler
10. William Griffiths

10 PLAYERS WHO HAVE MADE THE MOST APPEARANCES FOR MANCHESTER UNITED

1. Bobby Charlton   759
2. Bill Foulkes   688
3. Alex Stepney   539
4. Tony Dunne   535
5. Joe Spence   510
6. Arthur Albiston   482
7. George Best   466
8. Mark Hughes   462
9. Bryan Robson   456
10. Martin Buchan   456

10 MANCHESTER UNITED PLAYERS WHO HAVE MADE BETWEEN 300 AND 400 APPEARANCES FOR THE CLUB

1. Denis Law   399
2. Steve Coppell   395
3. Paddy Crerand   392
4. Nobby Stiles   392
5. Allenby Chilton   390
6. Mike Duxbury   376
7. Gary Bailey   373
8. Shay Brennan   355
9. Stan Pearson   345
10. Johnny Carey   344

Denis Law

10 MANCHESTER UNITED PLAYERS WHO MADE BETWEEN 400 AND 500 APPEARANCES FOR THE CLUB

1.	Arthur Albiston	482
2.	George Best	466
3.	Mark Hughes	460
4.	Bryan Robson	456
5.	Martin Buchan	455
6.	John Silcock	449
7.	Jack Rowley	422
8.	Sammy McIlroy	418
9.	Steve Bruce	409
10.	Lou Macari	400

THE ONLY PLAYER TO HAVE MADE MORE THAN 300 LEAGUE APPEARANCES FOR BOTH MANCHESTER CLUBS

1. Billy Meredith
   366 for Manchester City
   303 for Manchester United

10 PLAYERS WHO SPENT MORE THAN 10 YEARS AT OLD TRAFFORD AS A PLAYER

1.	Arthur Albiston	1974-88
2.	George Best	1963-74
3.	Shay Brennan	1957-70
4.	Martin Buchan	1971-83
5.	Johnny Carey	1937-53
6.	Bobby Charlton	1956-73
7.	Bill Foulkes	1952-70
8.	Clarence Hilditch	1919-32
9.	Denis Law	1962-73
10.	Bryan Robson	1981-94

Bryan Robson

10 PLAYERS WHO HAVE MADE MORE THAN 300 LEAGUE APPEARANCES FOR MANCHESTER UNITED

1. Bobby Charlton   606
2. Bill Foulkes   566
3. Joe Spence   481
4. Alex Stepney   433
5. John Silcock   423
6. Tony Dunne   414
7. Jack Rowley   380
8. Arthur Albiston   379
9. Martin Buchan   376
10. George Best   361

10 MORE PLAYERS WHO HAVE MADE MORE THAN 300 LEAGUE APPEARANCES FOR MANCHESTER UNITED

1. Allenby Chilton   353
2. Sammy McIlroy   320
3. Steve Coppell   320
4. Nobby Stiles   311
5. Lou Macari   311
6. Johnny Carey   306
7. Denis Law   305
8. Pat Crerand   304
9. Billy Meredith   303
10. Clarence Hilditch   301

10 MANCHESTER UNITED PLAYERS WHO HAVE RECEIVED A TESTIMONIAL MATCH

1. John Aston Snr.   v All-Stars XI
2. Bill Foulkes   v Manchester City
3. Bobby Charlton   v Glasgow Celtic
4. Denis Law   v Ajax Amsterdam
5. Tony Dunne   v Manchester City
6. Pat Crerand   v Man Utd XI 1968
7. Alex Stepney   v SL Benfica
8. John Sadler   v Preston North End
9. Sammy McIlroy   v FA Cup XI 1977
10. Don Givens   v Eire XI

Manchester United proudly showing off the FA Cup won for the first time in 1909.

10 PRE-WAR CAPTAINS OF NEWTON HEATH AND MANCHESTER UNITED

1. Sam Black   1883-87
2. Jack Powell   1887-90
3. Joe Cassidy   1892-93
4. Harry Stafford   1896-03
5. Charlie Roberts   1905-12
6. George Stacey   1912-14
7. George Hunter   1914-15
8. Frank Barson   1922-28
9. Jack Wilson   1928-32
10. Jimmy Brown   1935-39

10 POST WAR MANCHESTER UNITED CAPTAINS

1.	Johnny Carey	1945-53
2.	Stan Pearson	1953-54
3.	Roger Byrne	1955-58
4.	Bill Foulkes	1958-59
5.	Denis Law	1964-67
6.	Bobby Charlton	1967-73
7.	Martin Buchan	1975-82
8.	Bryan Robson	1982-94
9.	Steve Bruce	1994-96
10.	Eric Cantona	1996-97

10 PLAYERS WHO HAVE CAPTAINED MANCHESTER UNITED IN THE 1990s

1. Bryan Robson
2. Steve Bruce
3. Brian McClair
4. Mike Phelan
5. Paul Ince
6. Gary Pallister
7. Eric Cantona
8. Roy Keane
9. Peter Schmeichel
10. Denis Irwin

4 CHAMPIONSHIP MEDALS WON BY ERIC CANTONA IN CONSECUTIVE SEASONS

1.	French First Division	with Marseilles	1990-91
2.	English League Division 1	with Leeds United	1991-92
3.	FA Carling Premier League	with Manchester United	1992-93
4.	FA Carling Premier League	with Manchester United	1993-94

3 PROFESSIONAL FOOTBALLERS' ASSOCIATION AWARDS WON BY MARK HUGHES

1.	Young Player of the Year	1985
2.	Player of the Year	1989
3.	Player of the Year	1991

13 WINNERS' MEDALS WON BY DENIS IRWIN WITH MANCHESTER UNITED

1.	European Cup-Winners' Cup	1991
2.	European Super Cup	1991
3.	Rumbelows League Cup	1992
4.	FA Carling Premier League	1993
5.	FA Charity Shield	1993
6.	FA Carling Premier League	1994
7.	FA Cup	1994
8.	FA Charity Shield	1994
9.	FA Carling Premier League	1996
10.	FA Cup	1996
11.	FA Charity Shield	1996
12.	FA Carling Premier League	1997
13.	FA Charity Shield	1997

10 WINNERS' MEDALS WON BY GARY PALLISTER WITH MANCHESTER UNITED

1.	FA Cup	1990
2.	European Cup-Winners' Cup	1991
3.	European Super Cup	1991
4.	League Cup	1992
5.	FA Carling Premier League	1993
6.	FA Carling Premier League	1994
7.	FA Cup	1994
8.	FA Carling Premier League	1996
9.	FA Cup	1996
10.	FA Carling Premier League	1997

5 CUP COMPETITIONS IN WHICH DAVID HERD SCORED ON HIS COMPETITION DEBUT FOR MANCHESTER UNITED

1.	FA Cup	v Bolton Wanderers (h)	06.01.62
2.	European Cup-Winners' Cup	v Willem II Tilburg (a)	25.09.63
3.	Inter-Cities Fairs Cup	v Djurgardens IF (a)	23.09.64
4.	European Cup	v HJK Helsinki (a)	22.09.65
5.	Football League Cup	v Blackpool (a)	14.09.66

Herd scored in his second Football League game for United v Chelsea (h) on 23 August 1962

10 MANCHESTER UNITED PLAYERS WHO PLAYED IN A VICTORY INTERNATIONAL OR WARTIME INTER-LEAGUE MATCH

1.	Clarence Hilditch	for England	1919
2.	William Meredith	for Wales	1919
3.	Patrick O'Connell	for Ireland	1924
4.	Jack Rowley	for English League	1944
5.	Jimmy Delaney	for Scotland	1946
6.	Charlie Mitten	for England	1946
7.	John Warner	for Wales	1946
8.	Thomas Breen	for Ireland	1946
9.	Johnny Carey	for Ireland	1946
10.	Joseph Walton	for England	1946

THEIR DEBUT FOR THE CLUB AGAINST A TEAM THEY ALSO PLAYED FOR OR MANAGED

1.	George Graham	Arsenal
2.	Joe Jordan	Bristol City
3.	Albert Pape	Clapton Orient
4.	Brian Kidd	Everton
5.	William Hunter	Liverpool
6.	George Livingstone	Manchester City
7.	John Hall	Oldham Athletic
8.	Lou Macari	West Ham United
9.	Ian Greaves	Wolverhampton Wanderers
10.	Sammy McIlroy	Manchester City

3 MANCHESTER UNITED PLAYERS WHO LATER BECAME ASSISTANT MANAGERS AT THE CLUB

1. Paddy Crerand
2. Brian Kidd
3. Jim Ryan

4 MANCHESTER UNITED PLAYERS WHO HAVE MANAGED PRESTON NORTH END

1.	Bobby Charlton	May 1973 – August 1975
2.	Nobby Stiles	July 1977 – June 1981
3.	Brian Kidd	January 1986 – March 1986
4.	Sammy McIlroy	February 1990 – July 1991

10 PLAYERS WHO ALMOST BECAME A MANCHESTER UNITED PLAYER

1. **Alan Shearer (Southampton)** He joined Blackburn Rovers and later Newcastle United
2. **Marcello Salas (River Plate)** He joined SS Lazio
3. **Glenn Hoddle (Tottenham Hotspur)** He stayed at Tottenham Hotspur and later moved to Monaco
4. **Glenn Hysen** He joined Liverpool
5. **Gerry Francis (Queens Park Rangers)** He stayed at Queens Park Rangers
6. **David O'Leary** He was at Old Trafford for a trial but signed for Arsenal
7. **Phil Parkes (Queens Park Rangers)** He joined West Ham United
8. **Charlie Nicholas (Glasgow Celtic)** He joined Arsenal
9. **Miguel Nadal (FC Barcelona)** He stayed at FC Barcelona
10. **Mark Lawrenson (Brighton & Hove Albion)** He joined Liverpool

THE ONLY 6 PLAYERS TO HAVE WON TWO SETS OF ENGLISH DOUBLE WINNERS' MEDALS
(Medals won with Manchester United in Seasons 1993-94 and 1995-96)

1. Eric Cantona
2. Ryan Giggs
3. Denis Irwin
4. Roy Keane
5. Gary Pallister
6. Peter Schmeichel

3 MANCHESTER UNITED PLAYERS WHO HAVE WON THE PROFESSIONAL FOOTBALLERS' ASSOCIATION PLAYER OF THE YEAR AWARD

1. Mark Hughes   1989, 1991
2. Gary Pallister   1992
3. Eric Cantona   1994

4 MANCHESTER UNITED PLAYERS WHO HAVE WON THE PROFESSIONAL FOOTBALLERS' ASSOCIATION YOUNG PLAYER OF THE YEAR AWARD

1. Mark Hughes   1985
2. Lee Sharpe   1991
3. Ryan Giggs   1992 & 1993
4. David Beckham   1996

Andy Cole, then at Newcastle, won the award in 1994

4 MANCHESTER UNITED PLAYERS WHO HAVE WON THE FOOTBALL WRITERS' ASSOCIATION PLAYER OF THE YEAR AWARD

1. Johnny Carey   1949
2. Bobby Charlton   1966
3. George Best   1968
4. Eric Cantona   1996

10 MAJOR FOOTBALL HONOURS WON BY MANCHESTER UNITED PLAYERS

1.	1949 Football Writers' Association Player of the Year	Johnny Carey
2.	1964 European Footballer of the Year	Denis Law
3.	1966 Football Writers' Association Player of the Year	Bobby Charlton
4.	1966 European Footballer of the Year	Bobby Charlton
5.	1968 Football Writers' Association Player of the Year	George Best
6.	1968 European Footballer of the Year	George Best
7.	1989 PFA Player of the Year	Mark Hughes
8.	1991 PFA Player of the Year	Mark Hughes
9.	1992 PFA Player of the Year	Gary Pallister
10.	1996 Football Writers' Association Player of the Year	Eric Cantona

10 OTHER MAJOR FOOTBALL AWARDS WON BY PLAYERS WHO HAVE PLAYED FOR MANCHESTER UNITED

1.	1971 Scottish Footballer of the Year	Martin Buchan
2.	1980 Scottish Footballer of the Year	Gordon Strachan
3.	1985 PFA Young Player of the Year	Mark Hughes
4.	1987 Scottish Footballer of the Year	Brian McClair
5.	1991 PFA Young Player of the Year	Lee Sharpe
6.	1992 PFA Young Player of the Year	Ryan Giggs
7.	1993 PFA Young Player of the Year	Ryan Giggs
8.	1993 PFA Player of the Year	Paul McGrath
9.	1994 PFA Young Player of the Year	Andy Cole
10.	1994 PFA Player of the Year	Eric Cantona

3 FORMER SCOTTISH FOOTBALLERS OF THE YEAR WHO LATER SIGNED FOR MANCHESTER UNITED

1. Martin Buchan with Aberdeen   1971
2. Gordon Strachan with Aberdeen   1980
3. Brian McClair with Glasgow Celtic   1987

10 PLAYERS WHO HAVE LEFT OLD TRAFFORD TO JOIN A FOREIGN SIDE

1. Charlie Mitten — Bogota Sante Fe (Colombia)
2. Carlo Satori — Bologna (Italy)
3. Joe Jordan — AC Milan (Italy)
4. Gordon McQueen — Seiko (Hong Kong)
5. Jesper Olsen — Bordeaux (France)
6. Frank Stapleton — Ajax Amsterdam (Holland)
7. John Sivebaek — St. Etienne (France)
8. Ray Wilkins — AC Milan (Italy)
9. Arnold Muhren — Ajax Amsterdam (Holland)
10. Karel Poborsky — SL Benfica (Portugal)

10 PLAYERS WHO HAVE PLAYED FOR BOTH LEEDS UNITED AND MANCHESTER UNITED

1. Johnny Giles
2. Brian Greenhoff
3. Gordon McQueen
4. Joe Jordan
5. Peter Barnes
6. Andy Ritchie
7. Denis Irwin
8. Gordon Strachan
9. Eric Cantona
10. Lee Sharpe

10 PLAYERS WHO HAVE PLAYED FOR BOTH MANCHESTER UNITED AND MANCHESTER CITY

1. Billy Meredith
2. Sandy Turnbull
3. Denis Law
4. Ronald Wyn Davies
5. Brian Kidd
6. Sammy McIlroy
7. John Gidman
8. Peter Barnes
9. Tony Coton
10. Peter Beardsley

10 UNITED PLAYERS WHO HAVE HAD A BROTHER WHO HAS PLAYED LEAGUE FOOTBALL

1. Roger and Jack Doughty   (both played for Newton Heath)
2. Fred and Harry Erentz   (both played for Newton Heath)
3. James and John Hodge   (both played for United)
4. Jackie Blanchflower   (Danny played for Spurs)
5. Bobby Charlton   (Jack played for Leeds United)
6. Martin and George Buchan   (both played for United)
7. Jimmy and Brian Greenhoff   (both played for United)
8. Bryan Robson   (Gary played for West Brom Albion)
9. Danny Wallace   (Rod & Ray played for Southampton)
10. Gary and Philip Neville   (both play for United)

THE 10 OLDEST PLAYERS TO HAVE PLAYED FOR UNITED

1. Billy Meredith   48y, 285d   v Derby County (h) on 7 May 1921
2. Frank Mann   38y, 240d   v Sheff Wed (a) on 16 November 1929
3. John Jack Warner   38y, 213d   v Newcastle Utd (a) on 22 April 1950
4. Thomas Jones   38y, 5d   v Bradford P Ave. (a) on 11 Dec 1937
5. Edward Partridge   37y, 322d   v Aston Villa (h) on 1 January 1929
6. George Livingstone   37y, 313d   v Aston Villa (h) on 14 March 1914
7. Clarence Hilditch   37y, 243d   v Nottingham Forest (h) on 30 Jan 1932
8. Bill Foulkes   37y, 222d   v Southampton (h) on 16 August 1969
9. Bryan Robson   37y, 117d   v Coventry City (h) on 8 May 1994
10. Jack Hacking   37y, 42d   v Norwich City (a) on 2 February 1935

10 PLAYERS WHO MADE THEIR DEBUTS FOR UNITED BEFORE THEIR 18TH BIRTHDAY

1. Jeff Whitefoot   16 years
2. Duncan Edwards   16 years
3. Willie Anderson   16 years
4. Norman Whiteside   16 years
5. Sammy McIlroy   16 years
6. Ray Morton   16 years
7. George Best   17 years
8. Ryan Giggs   17 years
9. David Beckham   17 years
10. Nicky Butt   17 years

Ryan Giggs

Eric Cantona and Peter Schmeichel.

10 FOREIGN PLAYERS WHO HAVE PLAYED FOR UNITED

1.	Eric Cantona	France
2.	Nikola Jovanovic	Yugoslavia
3.	Peter Schmeichel	Denmark
4.	Arnold Muhren	Holland
5.	Ole Gunnar Solskjaer	Norway
6.	Karel Poborsky	Czech Republic
7.	Andrei Kanchelskis	Russia
8.	Jesper Olsen	Denmark
9.	Mark Bosnich	Australia
10.	William Prunier	France

10 BLACK PLAYERS WHO HAVE PLAYED FOR UNITED

1. Dennis Walker (Forward 1962-63)
2. Remi Moses (Midfielder 1981-88)
3. Paul McGrath (Defender 1982-89)
4. Laurie Cunningham (Forward 1982-83)
5. Viv Anderson (Full-Back 1987-91)
6. Paul Ince (Midfielder 1989-95)
7. Danny Wallace (Forward 1989-93)
8. Paul Parker (Full-Back 1991-96)
9. Dion Dublin (Forward 1992-94)
10. Andy Cole (Forward 1995-)

6 GRADUATES WHO HAVE PLAYED FOR MANCHESTER UNITED

1.	Gary Bailey	Witts University, South Africa	Physics
2.	Warren Bradley	Durham University	General Studies
3.	Steve Coppell	Liverpool University	Economics
4.	Alan Gowling	Manchester University	Economics
5.	Kevin Moran	University College, Dublin	Commerce
6.	Mike Pinner	Cambridge University	Law

10 PLAYERS VOTED BY MANCHESTER UNITED SUPPORTERS AS THE CLUB'S PLAYER OF THE YEAR

1. 1988   Brian McClair
2. 1989   Bryan Robson
3. 1990   Gary Pallister
4. 1991   Mark Hughes
5. 1992   Brian McClair
6. 1993   Paul Ince
7. 1994   Eric Cantona
8. 1995   Andrei Kanchelskis
9. 1996   Eric Cantona
10. 1997   David Beckham

4 OTHER TEAMS MARK HUGHES PLAYED FOR

1. Barcelona
2. Bayern Munich (loan)
3. Chelsea
4. Southampton

10 OTHER CLUBS GEORGE BEST PLAYED FOR

1. Hibernian
2. Dunstable Town
3. Stockport County
4. Fulham
5. Los Angeles Aztecs (USA)
6. Fort Lauderdale Strikers (USA)
7. Cork (Eire)
8. AFC Bournemouth
9. San Jose Earthquakes (USA)
10. Brisbane Lions (Australia)

Mark Hughes

10 CLUBS MICK MARTIN PLAYED FOR

1. Manchester United
2. Home Farm (Eire)
3. Bohemians (Eire)
4. West Bromwich Albion
5. Newcastle United
6. Vancouver Whitecaps (Canada)
7. Willingdon F.C.
8. Cardiff City
9. Peterborough United
10. Rotherham United

10 OTHER CLUBS TED MacDOUGALL PLAYED FOR

1. Liverpool
2. York City
3. Bournemouth & Biscombe Athletic
4. West Ham United
5. Norwich City
6. Southampton
7. Detroit Express (USA)
8. Poole Town
9. Totton
10. Athena (Australia)

10 OTHER CLUBS GORDON HILL PLAYED FOR

1. Staines Town
2. Southall
3. Millwall
4. Chicago Sting (USA)
5. Derby County
6. Queens Park Rangers
7. Montreal Manic (Canada)
8. New York Arrows (USA)
9. Kansas Comets (USA)
10. Tacoma Stars (USA)

10 OTHER CLUBS RONALD WYN DAVIES PLAYED FOR

1. Wrexham
2. Bolton Wanderers
3. Newcastle United
4. Manchester City
5. Blackpool
6. Crystal Palace (on loan)
7. Stockport County
8. Arcadia Shepherds (South Africa)
9. Crewe Alexandria
10. Bangor City

10 OTHER CLUBS RONALD TUDOR DAVIES PLAYED FOR

1. Chester
2. Luton Town
3. Norwich City
4. Southampton
5. Portsmouth
6. Arcadia Shepherd (South Africa)
7. Los Angeles Aztecs (USA)
8. Dorchester Town
9. Tulsa Roughnecks (USA)
10. Seattle Sounders (USA)

10 OTHER CLUBS GERRY DALY PLAYED FOR

1. Bohemians (Eire)
2. Derby County
3. New England Tea Men (on loan – USA)
4. Coventry City
5. Leicester City (on loan)
6. Birmingham City
7. Shrewsbury Town
8. Stoke City
9. Doncaster Rovers
10. Telford

10 OTHER CLUBS LAWRIE CUNNINGHAM PLAYED FOR

1. Orient
2. West Bromwich Albion
3. Real Madrid (Spain)
4. Sporting Gijon (Spain)
5. Olympique Marseilles (France)
6. Leicester City (on loan)
7. Rayo Vallecano (Spain)
8. F.C. Betis (Spain)
9. RSC Charleroi (Belgium)
10. Wimbledon (non-contract)

10 OTHER CLUBS ALAN BRAZIL PLAYED FOR

1. Ipswich Town
2. Detroit Express (USA)
3. Tottenham Hotspur
4. Coventry City
5. Queens Park Rangers
6. Witham Town
7. Chelmsford City
8. F.C. Baden (Switzerland)
9. Bury Town
10. Southend Manor

10 OTHER CLUBS PETER BARNES PLAYED FOR

1. Manchester City
2. West Bromwich Albion
3. Leeds United
4. Real Betis (on loan – Spain)
5. Melbourne J.U.S.T. (Australia)
6. Coventry City
7. Drogheda United (Eire)
8. Sporting Farense (Portugal)
9. Tampa Bay Rowdies (USA)
10. Cliftonville (Northern Ireland)

10 MANCHESTER UNITED PLAYERS WHO WERE LENT BY THE CLUB TO ANOTHER LEAGUE CLUB

1. David Beckham — Preston North End
2. Russell Beardsmore — Blackburn Rovers
3. William Garton — Birmingham City
4. Graeme Hogg — West Bromwich Albion
5. Jim Holton — Sunderland
6. Jim Leighton — Arsenal
7. Scott McGarvey — Wolverhampton Wanderers
8. Ralph Milne — West Ham United
9. Gary Walsh — Airdrieonians
10. Neil Whitworth — Preston North End

6 OTHER TEAMS ERIC CANTONA PLAYED FOR

1. Auxerre
2. Bordeaux
3. Olympique Marseille
4. Montpellier
5. Nimes
6. Leeds United

3 OTHER TEAMS DENIS LAW PLAYED FOR

1. Huddersfield Town
2. Manchester City
3. Torino

6 OTHER TEAMS SAMMY McILROY PLAYED FOR

1. Stoke City
2. Manchester City
3. Orgyte (Sweden) on loan
4. Bury
5. Modling
6. Preston North End

GOALKEEPERS

10 FAMOUS UNITED GOALKEEPERS

1.	Harry Moger	266 games	1903-12
2.	Jack Mew	199 games	1913-26
3.	Alf Steward	326 games	1921-32
4.	Jack Crompton	211 games	1945-55
5.	Ray Wood	208 games	1949-58
6.	David Gaskell	120 games	1956-66
7.	Harry Gregg	247 games	1957-66
8.	Alex Stepney	539 games	1966-78
9.	Gary Bailey	375 games	1978-87
10.	Peter Schmeichel	current	1991-99

Harry Gregg

13 GOALKEEPERS WHO PLAYED FOR NEWTON HEATH

1.	Frank Barrett	1896-1900
2.	John Davies	1892-93
3.	William Douglas	1893-96
4.	Joseph Fall	1893-94
5.	James Garvey	1900-01
6.	William Gyves	1890-91
7.	Tom Hay	1889-90
8.	Joseph Ridgway	1895-98
9.	James Saunders	1901-03
10.	James Warner	1892-93
11.	Joseph Wetherell	1896-97
12.	James Whitehouse	1900-03
13.	Walter Whittaker	1895-96

5 GOALKEEPERS USED BY MANCHESTER UNITED DURING THE 1952-53 SEASON

1. Reg Allen
2. Johnny Carey
3. Jack Crompton
4. Les Olive
5. Ray Wood

5 MANCHESTER UNITED PLAYERS WHO HAVE PLAYED IN GOAL FOR MANCHESTER UNITED

1.	Jackie Blanchflower	v Aston Villa (FA Cup Final)	04.05.57
2.	Alex Dawson	v Tottenham Hotspur (h)	14.01.61
3.	David Herd	v Liverpool (h)	23.11.63
4.	David Sadler	v Arsenal (a)	22.08.70
5.	Brian Greenhoff	v Birmingham City (a)	19.08.75

3 MANCHESTER UNITED GOALKEEPERS WHO ONLY PLAYED ONE GAME FOR THE CLUB

1.	Billy Behan	v Bury (h)	03.03.34
2.	Anthony Hawksworth	v Blackpool (a)	27.10.56
3.	Ian Wilkinson	v Cambridge United (a)	09.10.91

Games 1 and 2 : English League Division 1

Game 3 : Football League Cup, Round 2, 2nd leg

3 GOALKEEPERS WHO HAVE SCORED FOR MANCHESTER UNITED

1.	Alex Stepney	3 goals	2 League and 1 Friendly
2.	Harry Gregg	1	Friendly
3.	Peter Schmeichel	1	UEFA Cup

A GOALKEEPER WHO SCORED A GOAL AGAINST MANCHESTER UNITED

1.	Pat Jennings (Spurs)	Charity Shield	at Old Trafford on 12.08.67

7 DIFFERENT COUNTRIES WHERE MANCHESTER UNITED GOALKEEPERS HAVE BEEN BORN

1. Australia (Mark Bosnich)
2. Denmark (Peter Schmeichel)
3. England (Alex Stepney)
4. Holland (Raimond Van Der Gouw)
5. Northern Ireland (Harry Gregg)
6. Republic of Ireland (Paddy Roche)
7. Scotland (Jim Leighton)

5 IRISH BORN GOALKEEPERS WHO HAVE PLAYED FOR MANCHESTER UNITED

1. William Behan 1933-34
2. Patrick Dunne 1964-66
3. John Feehan 1949-50
4. Harry Gregg 1957-67
5. Patrick Roche 1974-82

5 SCOTTISH BORN GOALKEEPERS WHO HAVE PLAYED FOR NEWTON HEATH/MANCHESTER UNITED

1. Frank Barrett 1896-1900 Newton Heath
2. William Douglas 1893-96 Newton Heath
3. Hugh Edmonds 1910-12 Manchester United
4. Jim Leighton 1988-90 Manchester United
5. Archibald Montgomery 1905-06 Manchester United

1 WELSH BORN GOALKEEPER WHO PLAYED FOR MANCHESTER UNITED

1. William John 1936-37

2 GOALKEEPERS WHO PLAYED FOR BOTH NEWTON HEATH AND MANCHESTER UNITED

1. James Saunders 1901-03
2. James Whitehouse 1900-03

41 ENGLISH BORN GOALKEEPERS WHO HAVE PLAYED FOR MANCHESTER UNITED

1.	Reg Allen	1950-55
2.	Gary Bailey	1978-86
3.	Hubert Birchenough	1902-03
4.	John Breedon	1935-40
5.	Herbert Bloomfield	1907-08
6.	Robert Brown	1947-8
7.	Arthur Chesters	1929-32
8.	Gordon Clayton	1956-7
9.	Clifford Collinson	1946-7
10.	John Connaughton	1971-2
11.	John Crompton	1946-56
12.	William Fielding	1946-7
13.	John David Gaskell	1957-67
14.	John Hacking	1933-5
15.	John Hall	1932-6
16.	Anthony Hawksworth	1956-7
17.	Charles Hillam	1933-4
18.	Joseph Lancaster	1949-50
19.	Leonard Langford	1934-6
20.	John Mew	1912-26
21.	Henry Moger	1903-12
22.	John Moody	1931-3
23.	Robert Leslie Olive	1952-3
24.	Stephen Pears	1984-5
25.	James Pegg	1947-8
26.	Kevin Pilkington	1994-8
27.	Michael Pinner	1960-61
28.	Lancelot Richardson	1925-9
29.	Jimmy Rimmer	1967-73
30.	Elijah Round	1909-10
31.	Ezra Royals	1911-14
32.	Les Sealey	1989-91 and 1993-94
33.	Alex Stepney	1966-78
34.	Alfred Steward	1920-32
35.	John Sutcliffe	1903-04
36.	Chris Turner	1985-8
37.	Robert Valentine	1904-06
38.	Gary Walsh	1986-95
39.	Jeff Wealands	1982-4
40.	Ian Wilkinson	1991-2
41.	Ray Wood	1949-59

3 NON-BRITISH BORN GOALKEEPERS WHO HAVE PLAYED FOR MANCHESTER UNITED

1.	Mark Bosnich	1989-91	Australia
2.	Peter Schmeichel	1991-99	Denmark
3.	Raimond Van Der Gouw	1996-99	Holland

3 DIFFERENT TEAMS DENIS LAW SCORED FOR AGAINST GORDON BANKS AT WEMBLEY

1.	for Manchester United v Leicester City	1963 FA Cup Final
2.	for Rest of the World v England	1963 Challenge Match
3.	for Scotland v England	1965 and 1967 Internationals

10 EVENTS IN MARCH

1. 2 MARCH 1980
President Sir Matt Busby
Sir Matt Busby was elected as the first ever President of Manchester United.

2. 4 MARCH 1995
Record Premier League victory
Manchester United 9   Ipswich Town 0
United recorded their biggest ever win in the Premier League, defeating Ipswich Town 9-0 at Old Trafford. Andy Cole scored 5 (the highest number of goals scored by a United player in a League game). Roy Keane, Mark Hughes (2) and Paul Ince were the other goal scorers. It was the third time United have recorded a 9-0 victory.

3. 9 MARCH 1895
Newton Heath hit 14 goals against Walsall Town Swifts
Newton Heath beat Walsall Town Swifts 14-0 at home in a League game. This score would still have been the biggest win in League history but Walsall complained about the state of the pitch and the result was nullified. The game was replayed and the Heathens won 9-0.

4. 9 MARCH 1966
El Beatle destroys Lisbon Eagles
Benfica 1   Manchester United 5
United travelled to Lisbon with a slender 3-2 advantage from the Home Leg of this European Cup quarter-final clash. Before the game kicked off Eusebio was presented with his European Player Of The Year Award on the pitch. Benfica were almost invincible at their Stadium of Light but George Best had a night to remember as he tore through the home defence time after time. United were three up after only sixteen minutes with Best netting twice and setting up John Connelly for the third. Benfica, the previous season's losing finalists, didn't know what had hit them and even the normally productive Eusebio had a quiet night. Benfica's only goal came from a Shay Brennan own goal but United added two more in the last 10 minutes of the game from Paddy Crerand and Bobby Charlton. At the end of the game the home fans hurled cushions on to the pitch in disgust at their side's inept performance.

5. 11 MARCH 1941
Old Trafford is bombed
Old Trafford was virtually demolished as Hitler's bombers targeted the vast Trafford Park industrial complex in an attempt to halt engineering production for Britain's war effort. The main stand was destroyed along with the dressing rooms and offices. United filed a claim with the War Damage Commission for reconstruction and were awarded £22,278. It took over eight years to rebuild the stadium and in the meantime United hired neighbours Manchester City's Maine Road Ground for around £5,000 a year plus a percentage of the gate receipts.

6. 14 MARCH 1914
United suffer their worst ever home defeat
Manchester United 0 Aston Villa 6
United suffered their worst ever home defeat when Aston Villa thrashed them 6-0 in a Division 1 game. Sixteen years later United were beaten at Old Trafford by the same score in another League game. United's Irish forward, Michael Hamill, missed the game against Aston Villa because he was playing for Ireland against Scotland in the final Home International game of 1914. Ireland drew 1-1 in Belfast and won the Home International Championship for the first time in their history.

7. 18 MARCH 1964
United's worst European defeat
Sporting Lisbon 5 Manchester United 0
United were hopeful of progressing to the semi-finals of the 1963-64 European Cup-Winners' Cup having won the Home Leg 4-1. However, in their quarter-final Second Leg tie in Lisbon, United were easily beaten. The Portuguese side won the tie 6-4 on aggregate.

8. 22 MARCH 1980
Victory for the Reds in the 100th Manchester League derby
Manchester United 1 Manchester City 0
The 100th Manchester League derby was played at Old Trafford. United won the game 1-0 thanks to a Mickey Thomas goal. A bumper crowd of 56,387 was in attendance.

9. 23 MARCH 1995
Alex Ferguson awarded the CBE and Eric Cantona is given a two week prison sentence
Alex Ferguson attended Buckingham Palace for his investiture and received the CBE from the Queen. After the ceremony a reporter asked Alex Ferguson for an interview and wanted to talk to him about former Glasgow Rangers player, Davy Cooper, who had died that morning. Alex, a close friend of Davy Cooper, was too distraught to talk about him. The reporter then wanted to talk to Alex about Eric Cantona who had been given a two week prison sentence earlier in the day. The news came as a shock to the United manager who said he wished to speak to the club before discussing the matter.

10. 25 MARCH 1939
Old Trafford's highest ever attendance
A massive 76,962 fans crammed into Old Trafford for the 1939 FA Cup Semi-Final tie between Wolverhampton Wanderers and Grimsby Town.

THE MANAGEMENT

10 MEN WHO HAVE MANAGED MANCHESTER UNITED

1.	Ernest Mangnall	1903-12
2.	' John Robson	1914-21
3.	Clarence Hilditch	1926-27
4.	Herbert Bamlett	1927-31
5.	Sir Matt Busby	1945-69 & 1970-71
6.	Frank OíFarrell	1971-72
7.	Tommy Docherty	1972-77
8.	Dave Sexton	1977-81
9.	Ron Atkinson	1981-86
10.	Alex Ferguson	1986-

10 UNITED PLAYERS WHO LATER BECAME MANAGERS

1.	Clarence Lal Hilditch	(United's only ever Player-Manager)
2.	Johnny Carey	(Blackburn Rovers)
3.	Bobby Charlton	(Preston North End)
4.	Nobby Stiles	(Preston North End)
5.	Noel Cantwell	(Coventry City)
6.	Lou Macari	(Swindon Town)
7.	Joe Jordan	(Bristol City)
8.	Steve Coppell	(Crystal Palace)
9.	Bryan Robson	(Middlesbrough)
10.	Gordon Strachan	(Coventry City)

10 MANCHESTER UNITED PLAYERS WHO LATER BECAME PLAYER-MANAGERS/COACHES

1.	Johnny Giles	Shamrock Rovers
2.	Fred Goodwin	Scunthorpe United
3.	Ted MacDougall	Blackpool
4.	Jim McCalliog	Lincoln City
5.	Bryan Robson	Middlesbrough
6.	Jack Rowley	Plymouth Argyle
7.	Frank Stapleton	Bradford City
8.	Gordon Strachan	Coventry City
9.	Dennis Viollet	Linfield
10.	Ray Wilkins	QPR

2 MEN WHO HAVE BEEN PRESIDENTS OF MANCHESTER UNITED

1.	John H. Davies	1909-19
2.	Sir Matt Busby CBE	1980-94

7 MEN WHO HAVE BEEN THE CHAIRMAN OF MANCHESTER UNITED

1.	John H. Davies	1902-27 (President 1909-19)
2.	W. R. Deakin	1909-19
3.	G. H. Lawton	1927-32
4.	James W. Gibson	1932-51
5.	Harold Hardman	1951-65
6.	Louis C. Edwards	1965-80
7.	Martin C. Edwards	1980-present

10 MANCHESTER UNITED PLAYERS WHO MANAGED ABROAD

1.	John Thomas Ball	Excelsior Roubaix (France)
2.	Noel Cantwell	New England Tea Men (USA)
3.	Tony Dunne	Stenjker (Norway)
4.	Bill Foulkes	Mazda (Japan)
5.	Johnny Giles	Vancouver Whitecaps (Canada)
6.	Fred Goodwin	Minnesota Kicks (USA)
7.	Harry Gregg	Kitan Sports Club (Kuwait)
8.	Jimmy Greenhoff	Toronto Blizzard (Canada)
9.	James Hayes	Wiener SV (Austria)
10.	Edward Lewis	Witts F.C. (South Africa)

10 MORE MANCHESTER UNITED PLAYERS WHO MANAGED ABROAD

1.	Neil McBain	Estudiantes de la Plata (Argentina)
2.	Wilf McGuinness	Aris Salonika (Greece)
3.	George McLachlan	Le Havre (France)
4.	Gordon McQueen	Seiko (Japan)
5.	John Mew	Lima F.C. (Peru)
6.	Nobby Stiles	Vancouver Whitecaps (Canada)
7.	John Sutcliffe	Arnhem (Holland)
8.	Ernest Taylor	New Brighton F.C. (New Zealand)
9.	Ian Ure	(coached in Iceland)
10.	Dennis Viollet	Washington Diplomats (USA)

10 SIR MATT BUSBY FACTS

1. He played for Manchester City & Liverpool.

2. In 1934 he won an FA Cup winners' medal with Manchester City.

3. He was Scotland's captain during World War II.

4. Although he only won one cap for his country, he also played in seven wartime internationals for Scotland.

5. He was appointed the manager of Manchester United on 15 February 1945.

6. United's 1948 FA Cup Final victory over Blackpool was the club's first trophy under his management.

7. He built 3 great sides at Old Trafford during his career (the team of the late 1940s, the Busby Babes during the 1950s and his European Cup winning team during the 1960s).

8. His right hand man at Old Trafford was Jimmy Murphy.

9. He was very badly injured in the 1958 Munich Air Disaster.

10. He managed Manchester United twice (1945-69 and 1970-71).

10 TROPHIES WON BY MANCHESTER UNITED UNDER SIR MATT BUSBY

1. FA Cup   1948
2. League Championship   1952
3. FA Charity Shield   1952
4. League Championship   1956
5. FA Charity Shield   1956
6. League Championship   1957
7. FA Cup   1963
8. League Championship   1965
9. League Championship   1967
10. European Cup   1968

10 ALEX FERGUSON FACTS

1. He is a successful racehorse owner.

2. He was sent off 7 times during his playing career.

3. He top scored for every club he played for.

4. His first signings when he became the Manchester United manager were Viv Anderson & Brian McClair.

5. He managed the Scotland national team at the 1986 World Cup Finals in Mexico.

6. He started his managerial career with Falkirk.

7. He used to be the Player-Manager of East Stirling.

8. He brought Archie Knox, his right hand man at Aberdeen, with him when he accepted the offer to manage United.

9. He became Scotland's most expensive player when Glasgow Rangers paid Dunfermline £55,000 for him.

10. He won the European Cup-Winners' Cup, European Super Cup, 3 Premier Leagues, 4 Scottish Cups and the League Cup during his 10 year reign as the manager of Aberdeen.

10 BRIAN KIDD FACTS

1. He was born in Collyhurst, Manchester on 29 May 1949.

2. He scored for United in their 1968 European Cup Final win over Benfica on his 19th birthday.

3. When he left United in 1974 he joined Arsenal.

4. He scored 70 goals for United in 255 appearances.

5. When he left Arsenal to join Manchester City he played alongside Joe Royle (current Manchester City manager).

6. He played under 4 different managers at Old Trafford (Sir Matt Busby, Wilf McGuinness, Frank O'Farrell and Tommy Docherty).

7. He also played for Everton & Bolton Wanderers.

8. He won 2 England caps (versus Northern Ireland & Ecuador in 1970).

9. During his Old Trafford career he was sent off once (versus Tottenham Hotspur on 13 January 1968 – along with Joe Kinnear, the current Wimbledon manager).

10. He was appointed assistant-manager to Alex Ferguson at United when Archie Knox moved to Glasgow Rangers.

ALEX FERGUSON'S FIRST 10 GAMES IN CHARGE OF MANCHESTER UNITED

1.	Oxford United (a)	0-2	08.11.86
2.	Norwich City (a)	0-0	15.11.86
3.	Queens Park Rangers (a)	1-0	22.11.86
4.	Wimbledon (a)	0-1	29.11.86
5.	Tottenham Hotspur (h)	3-3	07.12.86
6.	Aston Villa (a)	3-3	13.12.86
7.	Leicester City (a)	2-0	20.12.86
8.	Liverpool (a)	1-0	26.12.86
9.	Norwich City (h)	0-1	27.12.86
10.	Newcastle United (h)	4-1	01.01.87

All games were played in Football League Division 1

ALEX FERGUSON'S FIRST 10 VICTORIES AS MANAGER OF MANCHESTER UNITED

1.	Queens Park Rangers (h)	1-0	22.11.86
2.	Leicester City (h)	2-0	20.12.86
3.	Liverpool (a)	1-0	26.12.86
4.	Newcastle United (h)	4-1	01.01.87
5.	Manchester City (h)	1-0	10.01.87
6.	Arsenal (h)	2-0	24.01.87
7.	Watford (h)	3-1	14.02.87
8.	Manchester City (h)	2-0	07.03.87
9.	Nottingham Forest (h)	2-0	28.03.87
10.	Oxford United (h)	3-2	04.04.87

Games 1-4 and 6-10: English League Division 1   Game 5:   FA Cup, 3rd Round

ALEX FERGUSON'S FIRST 10 FA CUP GAMES AS MANAGER OF MANCHESTER UNITED

1.	Manchester City (h)	R3	1-0	10.01.87
2.	Coventry City (h)	R4	0-1	31.01.87
3.	Ipswich Town (a)	R3	2-1	10.01.88
4.	Chelsea (h)	R4	2-0	30.01.88
5.	Arsenal (a)	R5	1-2	20.02.88
6.	QPR (h)	R3	0-0	07.01.89
7.	QPR (a)	R3, Replay	2-2 (aet)	11.01.89
8.	QPR (h)	R3, 2nd Replay	3-0	23.01.89
9.	Oxford United (h)	R4	4-0	28.01.89
10.	AFC Bournemouth (a)	R5	1-1	18.02.89

ALEX FERGUSON'S FIRST 10 WINS IN FA CUP GAMES

1.	Manchester City (h)	R3	1-0	10.01.87
2.	Ipswich Town (a)	R3	2-1	10.01.88
3.	Chelsea (h)	R4	2-0	30.01.88
4.	Q P R (h)	R3, 2nd Replay	3-0	23.01.89
5.	Oxford United (h)	R4	4-0	28.01.89
6.	AFC Bournemouth (h)	R5, Replay	1-0	22.01.89
7.	Nottingham Forest (a)	R3	1-0	07.01.90
8.	Hereford United (a)	R4	1-0	28.01.90
9.	Newcastle United (a)	R5	3-2	18.02.90
10.	Sheffield United (a)	R6	1-0	11.03.90

MANCHESTER UNITED'S FIRST 10 GAMES IN EUROPEAN COMPETITION UNDER ALEX FERGUSON

1.	Pecsi Munkas (h)	R1, 1st Leg	2-0	19.09.90
2.	Pecsi Munkas (a)	R1, 2nd Leg	1-0	03.10.90
3.	Wrexham (h)	R2, 1st Leg	3-0	23.10.90
4.	Wrexham (a)	R2, 2nd Leg	2-0	07.11.90
5.	Montpellier (h)	R3, 1st Leg	1-1	06.03.91
6.	Montpellier (a)	R3, 2nd Leg	2-0	19.03.91
7.	Legia Warsaw (a)	SF, 1st Leg	3-1	10.04.91
8.	Legia Warsaw (h)	SF, 2nd Leg	1-1	24.04.91
9.	Barcelona (n)	Final	2-1	15.05.91
10.	PAE Athinaikos (a)	R1, 1st Leg	0-0	18.09.91

All games were played in the European Cup-Winners' Cup.
Game 9 was the 1991 Final which was played in Rotterdam, Holland.

ALEX FERGUSON'S FIRST 10 WINS IN EUROPEAN COMPETITION AS MANAGER OF MANCHESTER UNITED

1.	Pecsi Munkas (h)	R1, 1st Leg	2-0	19.09.90
2.	Pecsi Munkas (a)	R2, 2nd Leg	1-0	03.10.90
3.	Wrexham (h)	R2, 1st Leg	3-0	23.10.90
4.	Wrexham (a)	R2, 2nd Leg	2-0	07.11.90
5.	Montpellier (a)	R3, 2nd Leg	2-0	19.03.91
6.	Legia Warsaw (a)	SF, 1st Leg	3-1	10.04.91
7.	Barcelona (n)	Final	2-1	15.05.91
8.	PAE Athinaikos (h)	R1, 2nd Leg	2-0	02.10.91
9.	Kispest-Honved (a)	R1, 1st Leg	3-2	15.09.93
10.	Kispest-Honved (h)	R2, 2nd Leg	2-0	29.09.93

Games 1 and 8 were in the European Cup-Winners' Cup   Games 9 and 10 were in the European Cup

ALEX FERGUSON'S FIRST 10 LOSSES AS MANCHESTER UNITED MANAGER

1.	Oxford United (a)	0-2	08.11.86
2.	Wimbledon (a)	0-1	29.11.86
3.	Norwich City (h)	0-1	27.12.86
4.	Coventry City (h)	0-1	31.01.87
5.	Luton Town (a)	1-2	14.03.87
6.	Sheffield Wednesday (a)	0-1	21.03.87
7.	Newcastle United (a)	1-2	18.04.87
8.	Wimbledon (h)	0-1	02.05.87
9.	Tottenham Hotspur (a)	0-4	04.05.87
10.	Everton (a)	1-2	19.09.87

Games 1-3 and 5-10: English League Division 1   Game 4: FA Cup 4th Round

THE FIRST TEAM SELECTED BY ALEX FERGUSON AS MANCHESTER UNITED MANAGER
(Oxford United v Manchester United, Division One, 8 November 1986)

1. Chris Turner
2. Mike Duxbury
3. Arthur Albiston
4. Kevin Moran
5. Paul McGrath
6. Graeme Hogg
7. Clayton Blackmore
8. Remi Moses
9. Frank Stapleton
10. Peter Davenport
11. Peter Barnes
12. Jesper Olsen (for McGrath)

United lost 2-0.

Paul McGrath

ALEX FERGUSON'S FIRST 10 LEAGUE CUP GAMES AS MANCHESTER UNITED MANAGER

1.	Hull City (h)	5-0	R2, 1st Leg	23.09.87
2.	Hull City (a)	1-0	R2, 2nd Leg	07.10.87
3.	Crystal Palace (h)	2-1	R3	28.10.87
4.	Bury (a)	2-1	R4	18.11.87
5.	Oxford United (a)	0-2	R5	20.01.88
6.	Rotherham United (a)	1-0	R2, 1st Leg	28.09.88
7.	Rotherham United (h)	5-0	R2, 2nd Leg	12.10.88
8.	Wimbledon (a)	1-2	R3	02.11.88
9.	Portsmouth (a)	3-2	R2, 1st Leg	20.09.89
10.	Portsmouth (h)	0-0	R2, 2nd Leg	03.10.89

Although Game 4 was technically an away fixture, the tie was played at Old Trafford.

THE FIRST 10 PLAYERS TO SCORE FOR MANCHESTER UNITED UNDER THE MANAGEMENT OF ALEX FERGUSON

1.	John Sivebaek	v QPR (h)	22.11.86
2.	Peter Davenport	v Tottenham Hotspur (h)	07.12.86
3.	Norman Whiteside	above game	
4.	Colin Gibson	v Leicester City (h)	20.12.86
5.	Frank Stapleton	above game	
6.	Jesper Olsen	v Southampton (a)	03.01.87
7.	Gordon Strachan	v Arsenal (h)	24.01.87
8.	Terry Gibson	above game	
9.	Paul McGrath	v Watford (h)	14.02.87
10.	Bryan Robson	v Manchester City (h)	07.03.87

All games were in English League Division 1.

THE FIRST 10 PLAYERS TO BE GIVEN THEIR MANCHESTER UNITED DEBUT BY ALEX FERGUSON

1.	Gary Walsh	v Aston Villa (a)	13.12.86
2.	Liam OíBrien	v Leicester City (h)	20.12.86
3.	Anthony Gill	v Southampton (a)	03.01.87
4.	Nicholas Wood	v Nottingham Forest (h)	28.03.87
5.	Viv Anderson	v Southampton (a)	15.08.87
6.	Brian McClair	above game	
7.	Steve Bruce	v Portsmouth (a)	19.12.87
8.	Lee Martin	v Wimbledon (h)	09.05.88
9.	Jim Leighton	v Q P R (h)	27.08.88
10.	Lee Sharpe	v West Ham United (h)	24.09.88

All games were played in English League Division 1.

THE FIRST 10 TROPHIES WON BY MANCHESTER UNITED UNDER ALEX FERGUSON

1.	FA Cup	1990
2.	European Cup-Winners' Cup	1991
3.	European Super Cup	1991
4.	League Cup	1992
5.	FA Carling Premier League	1993
6.	FA Charity Shield	1993
7.	FA Carling Premier League	1994
8.	FA Cup	1994
9.	FA Charity Shield	1994
10.	FA Carling Premier League	1996

TOMMY DOCHERTY'S FIRST 10 GAMES AS MANAGER OF MANCHESTER UNITED

1.	Leeds United (h)	1-1	23.12.72
2.	Derby County (a)	1-3	26.12.72
3.	Arsenal (a)	1-3	06.01.73
4.	Wolverhampton Wanderers (a)	0-1	13.01.73
5.	West Ham United (h)	2-2	20.01.73
6.	Everton (h)	0-0	24.01.73
7.	Coventry City (a)	1-1	27.01.73
8.	Wolverhampton Wanderers (h)	2-1	10.02.73
9.	Ipswich Town (a)	1-4	17.02.73
10.	West Bromwich Albion (h)	2-1	03.03.73

Games 1-3: English League Division 1   Game 4: FA Cup, Round 3   Games 5 -10: English League Division 1

TOMMY DOCHERTY'S FIRST 10 WINS AS MANAGER OF MANCHESTER UNITED

1.	Wolverhampton Wanderers (h)	2-1	10.02.73
2.	West Bromwich Albion (h)	2-1	03.03.73
3.	Newcastle United (h)	2-1	17.03.73
4.	Southampton (a)	2-0	31.03.73
5.	Norwich City (h)	1-0	07.04.73
6.	Crystal Palace (h)	2-0	11.04.73
7.	Leeds United (a)	1-0	18.04.73
8.	Stoke City (h)	1-0	29.08.73
9.	Queens Park Rangers (h)	2-1	01.09.73
10.	West Ham United (h)	3-1	15.09.73

All games were played in English League Division 1

TOMMY DOCHERTY'S FIRST 10 LOSSES AS MANAGER OF MANCHESTER UNITED

1.	Derby County (a)	1-3	26.12.72
2.	Arsenal (a)	1-3	06.01.73
3.	Wolverhampton Wanderers (a)	0-1	13.01.73
4.	Ipswich Town (a)	1-4	17.02.73
5.	Birmingham City (a)	1-3	10.03.73
6.	Sheffield United (h)	1-2	23.04.73
7.	Chelsea (a)	0-1	28.04.73
8.	Arsenal (a)	0-1	25.08.73
9.	Leicester City (a)	0-1	05.09.73
10.	Ipswich Town (a)	1-2	08.09.73

Games 1-2:   English League Division 1

Game 3: FA Cup Round 3   Games 4-10: English League Division 1

TOMMY DOCHERTY'S FIRST 10 FA CUP GAMES AS MANAGER OF MANCHESTER UNITED

1.	Wolves (a)	R3	0-1	13.01.73
2.	Plymouth Argyle (h)	R3	1-0	05.01.74
3.	Ipswich Town (h)	R4	0-1	26.01.74
4.	Walsall (h)	R3	0-0	04.01.75
5.	Walsall (a)	R3 Replay	2-3 (aet)	07.01.75
6.	Oxford United (h)	R3	2-1	03.01.76
7.	Peterborough United (h)	R4	3-1	24.01.76
8.	Leicester City (a)	R5	2-1	14.02.76
9.	Wolves (h)	R6	1-1	06.03.76
10.	Wolves (a)	R6 Replay	3-2 (aet)	09.03.76

TOMMY DOCHERTY'S FIRST 10 FA CUP WINS AS MANAGER OF MANCHESTER UNITED

1.	Plymouth Argyle (h)	R3	1-0	05.01.74
2.	Oxford United (h)	R3	2-1	03.01.76
3.	Peterborough United (h)	R4	3-1	24.01.76
4.	Leicester City (a)	R5	2-1	14.02.76
5.	Wolves (a)	R6 Replay	3-2 (aet)	09.03.76
6.	Derby County (n)	Semi-Final	2-0	03.04.76
7.	Walsall (h)	R3	1-0	08.01.77
8.	QPR (h)	R4	1-0	29.01.77
9.	Southampton (h)	R5 Replay	2-1	08.03.77
10.	Aston Villa (h)	R6	2-1	19.03.77

Game no. 5 was played at Hillsborough, Sheffield

THE FIRST TEAM SELECTED BY TOMMY DOCHERTY AS MANAGER OF MANCHESTER UNITED

(Manchester United v Leeds United, Division 1, 23 December 1972)

1. Alex Stepney
2. Thomas O'Neill
3. Tony Dunne
4. Willie Morgan
5. David Sadler
6. Martin Buchan
7. Ronald Wyn Davies
8. Ted MacDougall
9. Bobby Charlton
10. Denis Law
11. Ian Storey-Moore
12. Brian Kidd (for Law)

The game was drawn 1-1 (scorer: MacDougall)

Tommy Docherty

FIRST 10 MANCHESTER UNITED PLAYERS TO SCORE UNDER TOMMY DOCHERTY

1.	Ted MacDougall	v Leeds United (h)	23.12.72
2.	Ian Storey-Moore	v Derby County (a)	26.12.72
3.	Brian Kidd	v Arsenal (a)	06.01.73
4.	Bobby Charlton	v West Ham United (h)	20.01.73
5.	Lou Macari	v West Ham United (h)	20.01.73
6.	Jim Holton	v Coventry City (a)	24.01.73
7.	Mick Martin	v Newcastle United (h)	17.03.73
8.	George Graham	v Tottenham Hotspur (a)	24.03.73
9.	Willie Morgan	v Crystal Palace (h)	11.04.73
10.	Trevor Anderson	v Leeds United (a)	18.04.73

THE FIRST 10 PLAYERS PURCHASED BY TOMMY DOCHERTY FOR MANCHESTER UNITED

1.	George Graham	from	Arsenal
2.	Alex Forsyth	from	Partick Thistle
3.	Lou Macari	from	Glasgow Celtic
4.	Jim Holton	from	Shrewsbury Town
5.	Mick Martin	from	Bohemians
6.	Ray O'Brien	from	Shelbourne
7.	Gerry Daly	from	Bohemians
8.	Paddy Roche	from	Shelbourne
9.	Jim McCalliog	from	Wolverhampton Wanderers
10.	Stuart Pearson	from	Hull City

THE FIRST 10 UNITED PLAYERS SOLD BY TOMMY DOCHERTY

1. Ted MacDougall   to   West Ham United
2. Paul Edwards   to   Oldham Athletic
3. Carlo Sartori   to   Bologna
4. Wyn Davies   to   Blackpool
5. David Sadler   to   Preston North End
6. Jimmy Rimmer   to   Arsenal
7. Ray O'Brien   to   Notts County
8. Peter Fletcher   to   Hull City
9. George Buchan   to   Bury
10. Brian Kidd   to   Arsenal

FIRST 10 PLAYERS GIVEN THEIR MANCHESTER UNITED DEBUT BY TOMMY DOCHERTY

1. George Graham   v Arsenal (a)   06.01.73
2. Alex Forsyth   v Arsenal (a)   06.01.73
3. Jim Holton   v West Ham United (h)   20.01.73
4. Lou Macari   v West Ham United (h)   20.01.73
5. Mick Martin   v Everton (h)   24.01.73
6. Trevor Anderson   v Southampton (a)   31.03.73
7. Peter Fletcher   v Stoke City (a)   14.04.73
8. Arnold Sidebottom   v Sheffield United (h)   23.04.73
9. Gerry Daly   v Arsenal (a)   25.08.73
10. Brian Greenhoff   v Ipswich Town (a)   08.09.73

MANCHESTER UNITED'S FIRST 10 LEAGUE CUP GAMES UNDER TOMMY DOCHERTY

1. Middlesbrough (h)   R2   0-1   08.10.73
2. Charlton Athletic (a) R2   5-1   11.09.74
3. Manchester City (h)   R3   1-0   09.10.74
4. Burnley (h)   R4   3-2   13.11.74
5. Middlesbrough (a)   R5   0-0   04.12.74
6. Middlesbrough (h)   R5 Replay   3-0   18.12.74
7. Norwich City (h)   SF 1st leg 2-2   15.01.75
8. Norwich City (a)   SF 2nd leg 0-1   22.01.75
9. Brentford (h)   R2   2-1   10.09.75
10. Aston Villa (a)   R3   2-1   08.10.75

MANCHESTER UNITED'S ONLY LEAGUE CUP VICTORIES UNDER TOMMY DOCHERTY

1.	Charlton Athletic (a)	R2	5-1	11.09.74
2.	Manchester City (h)	R3	1-0	09.10.74
3.	Burnley (h)	R4	3-2	13.11.74
4.	Middlesbrough (h)	R5 Replay	3-0	18.12.74
5.	Brentford (h)	R2	2-1	10.09.75
6.	Aston Villa (a)	R3	2-1	08.10.75
7.	Tranmere Rovers (h)	R2	5-0	01.09.76
8.	Sunderland (h)	R3 2nd Replay	1-0	06.10.76
9.	Newcastle United (h)	R4	7-2	27.10.76

RON ATKINSON'S FIRST 10 GAMES IN CHARGE OF MANCHESTER UNITED

1.	Coventry City (a)	1-2	29.08.81
2.	Nottingham Forest (h)	0-0	31.08.81
3.	Ipswich Town (h)	1-2	05.09.81
4.	Aston Villa (a)	1-1	12.09.81
5.	Swansea City (h)	1-0	19.09.81
6.	Middlesbrough (a)	2-0	22.09.81
7.	Arsenal (a)	0-0	26.09.81
8.	Leeds United (h)	1-0	30.09.81
9.	Wolverhampton Wanderers (h)	5-0	03.10.81
10.	Tottenham Hotspur (a)	0-1	07.10.81

Games 1-9: English League Division 1

Game 10: League Cup, 2nd Round, 1st leg

MANCHESTER UNITED'S FIRST 10 WINS UNDER RON ATKINSON

1.	Swansea City (h)	1-0	19.09.81
2.	Middlesbrough (a)	2-0	22.09.81
3.	Leeds United (h)	1-0	30.09.81
4.	Wolverhampton Wanderers (h)	5-0	03.10.81
5.	Middlesbrough (h)	1-0	21.10.81
6.	Liverpool (a)	2-1	24.10.81
7.	Notts County (h)	2-1	31.10.81
8.	Sunderland (a)	5-1	07.11.81
9.	Brighton & Hove Albion (h)	2-0	28.11.81
10.	Stoke City (a)	3-0	23.01.82

All games were played in English League Division 1

MANCHESTER UNITED'S FIRST 10 LOSSES UNDER RON ATKINSON

1.	Coventry City (a)	1-2	29.08.81
2.	Ipswich Town (h)	1-2	05.09.81
3.	Tottenham Hotspur (a)	0-1	07.10.81
4.	Tottenham Hotspur (h)	0-1	28.10.81
5.	Tottenham Hotspur (a)	1-3	21.11.81
6.	Southampton (a)	2-3	05.12.81
7.	Watford (a)	0-1	02.01.82
8.	Swansea City (a)	0-2	30.01.82
9.	Coventry City (h)	0-1	17.03.82
10.	Liverpool (h)	0-1	07.04.82

Games 1-3 : English League Division 1

Game 4: League Cup, 2nd Round, 2nd leg

Games 5-6: English League Division 1

Game 7: FA Cup 3rd Round

Games 8-10: English League Division 1

THE FIRST 10 MANCHESTER UNITED PLAYERS TO SCORE UNDER RON ATKINSON

1.	Lou Macari	v Coventry City (a)	29.08.81
2.	Frank Stapleton	v Ipswich Town (h)	05.09.81
3.	Garry Birtles	v Swansea City (h)	19.09.81
4.	Sammy McIlroy	v Wolverhampton Wanderers (h)	03.10.81
5.	Steve Coppell	v Birmingham City (h)	17.10.81
6.	Remi Moses	v Middlesbrough (h)	21.10.81
7.	Kevin Moran	v Liverpool (a)	24.10.81
8.	Arthur Albiston	v Liverpool (a)	24.10.81
9.	Bryan Robson	v Sunderland (a)	07.11.81
10.	Ashley Grimes	v Everton (a)	10.04.82

All games were played in English League Division 1

THE FIRST TEAM SELECTED BY RON ATKINSON AS MANAGER OF MANCHESTER UNITED
(Coventry City v Manchester United, Division 1, 29 August 1981)

1. Gary Bailey
2. John Gidman
3. Arthur Albiston
4. Ray Wilkins
5. Gordon McQueen
6. Martin Buchan
7. Steve Coppell
8. Garry Birtles
9. Frank Stapleton
10. Lou Macari
11. Sammy McIlroy
12. Jimmy Nicholl (not used)

United lost 1-2 (scorer: Macari)

THE FIRST 10 PLAYERS TO BE GIVEN THEIR MANCHESTER UNITED DEBUT BY RON ATKINSON

1.	John Gidman	v Coventry City (a)	29.08.91
2.	Frank Stapleton	v Coventry City (a)	29.08.91
3.	Remi Moses	v Swansea City (h)	19.09.81
4.	Bryan Robson	v Tottenham Hotspur (a)	07.10.81
5.	Norman Whiteside	v Brighton & Hove Albion (a)	24.04.82
6.	Alan Davies	v Southampton (h)	01.05.82
7.	Arnold Muhren	v Birmingham City (h)	28.08.82
8.	Peter Beardsley	v AFC Bournemouth (h)	06.10.82
9.	Paul McGrath	v Tottenham Hotspur (h)	13.11.82
10.	Jeff Wealands	v Coventry City (h)	02.04.83

Games 1-3: English League Division 1

Game 4: League Cup, 2nd Round, 1st leg

Games 5-7: English League Division 1

Game 8: League Cup, 2nd Round, 1st leg

Games 9-10: English League Division 1

4 MANCHESTER UNITED PLAYERS WHO LATER BECAME DIRECTORS AT THE CLUB

1. Harry Stafford
2. Harold Hardman
3. Les Olive
4. Bobby Charlton

5 OCCASIONS WHEN THE MANCHESTER UNITED MANAGER WAS AWARDED THE MANAGER OF THE YEAR AWARD

1.	Matt Busby	1968
2.	Alex Ferguson	1993
3.	Alex Ferguson	1994
4.	Alex Ferguson	1996
5.	Alex Ferguson	1997

3 TEAMS MANAGED BY MATT BUSBY

1.	Manchester United	1945-69 & 1970-71
2.	British Olympic Team	1948
3.	Scotland	1958

2 POST-WAR MANCHESTER UNITED PLAYERS WHO HAVE SPENT TWO DIFFERENT PERIODS WITH THE CLUB

1.	Mark Hughes	1983-86 and 1988-95
2.	Les Sealey	1990-91 and 1993-94

A MANCHESTER UNITED MANAGER WHO WON BOTH THE PREMIER LEAGUE TITLES OF ENGLAND AND SCOTLAND

1. Alex Ferguson   with Aberdeen and Manchester United 1993, 1994, 1996 and 1997

5 MANAGERS WHO HAVE LED MANCHESTER UNITED TO CHAMPIONSHIP SUCCESS

1.	Ernest Mangnall	Division 1	1908 and 1911
2.	A. Scott Duncan	Division 2	1936
3.	Matt Busby	Division 1	1952, 1956, 1957, 1965 and 1967
4.	Tommy Docherty	Division 2	1975
5.	Alex Ferguson	Premier League	1993, 1994, 1996, 1997

1 MANCHESTER UNITED PLAYER-MANAGER

1. Clarence Lal Hilditch   1926-27

Wilf McGuinness both played for and managed Manchester United but he was never their Player-Manager

5 MANAGERS WHO HAVE LED MANCHESTER UNITED TO FA CUP SUCCESS

1. Ernest Mangnall   1909
2. Matt Busby   1948 and 1963
3. Tommy Docherty   1977
4. Ron Atkinson   1983 and 1985

6 DIFFERENT CUPS WON BY ALEX FERGUSON

1. Scottish Cup   with Aberdeen
2. Scottish League Cup   with Aberdeen
3. European Cup-Winners' Cup   with Aberdeen and Manchester United
4. English FA Cup   with Manchester United
5. European Super Cup   with Aberdeen and Manchester United
6. English League Cup   with Manchester United

1 MANCHESTER UNITED MANAGER WHO USED TO BE A REFEREE

1. Herbert Bamlett   Manager   1927-31

Bamlett refereed the 1914 FA Cup Final at Crystal Palace

1 MANCHESTER UNITED MANAGER WHO ALSO MANAGED THE WELSH NATIONAL TEAM

1. Jimmy Murphy   Manager February 1958 – August 1958

Murphy managed Wales in the 1958 World Cup Finals in Sweden

Big Ron with his FA Cup winning team in 1983.

5 MANCHESTER UNITED MANAGERS WHO WON THE FA CHARITY SHIELD

1.	Ernest Mangnall	1908 & 1911
2.	Matt Busby	1952, 1956, 1957, 1965 (joint) and 1967 (joint)
3.	Tommy Docherty	1977 (joint)
4.	Ron Atkinson	1983
5.	Alex Ferguson	1990 (joint), 1993. 1994, 1996 and 1997

1 MAN WHO MANAGED NEWTON HEATH IN THE FOOTBALL ALLIANCE, DIVISION 1 AND DIVISION 2

1.	A. H. Albut	Football Alliance	1889-92
		Division 1	1892-94
		Division 2	1894-1900

2 MEN WHO MANAGED NEWTON HEATH IN DIVISION 2

1. A. H. Albut   1894-1900
2. James West   1900-02

1 MAN WHO MANAGED BOTH NEWTON HEATH AND MANCHESTER UNITED

1. James West   Newton Heath   1900-02

    Manchester United   1902-03

6 MEN WHO HAVE MANAGED MANCHESTER UNITED IN DIVISION 2

1. James West   1902-03
2. Ernest Mangnall   1903-06
3. John Chapman   1922-25
4. Walter Crickmer   1931-32 and 1937-38
5. A. Scott Duncan   1932-36
6. Tommy Docherty   1974-75

5 MEN WHO MANAGED MANCHESTER UNITED IN DIVISIONS 1 AND 2

1.	Ernest Mangnall	Division 2	1903-06
		Division 1	1906-12
2.	John Chapman	Division 1	1921-22 and 1925- Oct 1926
		Division 2	1922-25
3.	A. Scott Duncan	Division 2	1932-36
		Division 1	1936-Nov 1937
4.	Walter Crickmer	Division 2	1931-32 and 1937-38
		Division 1	1938-39
5.	Tommy Docherty	Division 1	Dec 1972-74 and 1975-77
		Division 2	1974-75

2 MEN WHO HAVE HAD TWO SPELLS AS MANAGER OF MANCHESTER UNITED

1. Walter Crickmer   1931-32 and 1937-45
2. Matt Busby   1945-69 and 1970-71

10 EVENTS IN APRIL

1. 4 APRIL 1953
Duncan Edwards Makes His Debut
Manchester United 1 Cardiff City 4
When Duncan Edwards was only 11 years old he played in the Dudley Boys Team whose players had an average age of 15. Matt Bubsy travelled to Dudley and signed the young Edwards just two hours into his sixteenth birthday. Duncan made his United debut aged 16 years, 185 days and made his full England debut aged 18 years, 183 days (England beat Scotland 7-2). With the Reds Duncan won three FA Youth Cup Winners' medals, two Championship medals (1956 and 1957) and appeared in the 1957 FA Cup Final loss to Aston Villa. Tragically he lost his life in the Munich air disaster when he was only 21.

2. 5 APRIL 1941
United lose opening game at their new adopted home
Manchester United 2 Blackpool 3
Severe bomb damage to Old Trafford on the night of 11 March 1941 resulted in United having to use neighbours, City's, Maine Road ground until 24 August 1949. The Seasiders won 3-2 (scorers: Mears and Smith).

3. 7 APRIL 1956
Busby Babes clinch their first title
Manchester United 2 Blackpool 1
In front of their biggest crowd of the season, 62,277, United beat Blackpool 2-1 (scorers: Bery and Taylor) at Old Trafford to win the First Division Championship for the fourth time in the Club's history. United's superb League form at the turn of the year was instrumental in their Championship success. In the second half of the season the Reds lost only one of their final sixteen league games.

4. 10 APRIL 1993
Bruce double strike late in injury time seals victory
Manchester United 2 Sheffield Wednesday 1
This win was possibly the one which destined United to capture their first Championship for 26 years. Trailing 1-0, the game went into injury time. Steven Bruce scored two headers for the Reds in the seven minutes of injury time, the second of which resulted in Alex Ferguson and Brian Kidd running excitedly on to the Old Trafford pitch.

5. 10 APRIL 1994
The goal that inspired the Double
Manchester United 1 Oldham Athletic 1
United met Oldham Athletic at Wembley in the FA Cup semi-final and after 90 minutes the game was scoreless. In the first minute of the second period of injury time Neil Pointon scored for Oldham and United's dreams of winning the Double were fast disappearing. United's entire season, after their League Cup final defeat two weeks earlier, was on the line, but cometh the hour, cometh the man. With a minute of the game remaining, Brian McClair headed the ball into the Oldham box where Mark Hughes met it on the volley and sent it scorching past a dumbstruck John Hallworth and into the Oldham goal. United were let off the hook and after easily disposing of Oldham in the replay, went on to retain their Premiership crown and win the coveted Double.

6. 14 APRIL 1941
Reds inflict Blues' heaviest home defeat
Manchester City 1 Manchester United 7
In a North Regional 2nd Competition game the Reds defeated City 7-1 (scorers: Rowley 4, Pearson 2 and Smith) at Maine Road. It was Manchester City's heaviest defeat at Maine Road since the ground was first opened in 1923.

7. 19 APRIL 1997
Liverpool 1 Manchester United 3
United came to Anfield knowing that a win over Liverpool would virtually assure them of winning their fourth Premiership crown in five seasons. In a pulsating game the Reds didn't disappoint Fergie's travelling Red and White Army, playing with the authority of Champions and winning the game 3-1. Gary Pallister scored two bullet-like headers direct from corner kicks and Andy Cole sealed victory with United's third goal. David James had a nightmare of a game in goal for Liverpool.

8. 24 APRIL 1909
First FA Cup Success
Manchester United 1 Bristol City 0
Sandy Turnbull scored the only goal of the game in the 22nd minute to give United their first ever FA Cup win. Billy Meredith was the man of the match, adding this medal to the one he won with Manchester City in 1904. Charlie Roberts, the United captain proudly collected the Cup from Lord Charles Beresford. The United team for the Final, played at the Crystal Palace stadium lined up as follows: Moger, Stacey, Hayes, Duckworth, Roberts, Bell, Meredith, Halse, Turnbull J, Turnbull A, Wall.

9. 27 APRIL 1974
Law's back-heeled goal helps relegate United
Manchester United 0 Manchester City 1
On the last Saturday of the 1973-74 season United faced Manchester City in a game which could decide whether or not the Reds would be playing Second Division football the following season. Denis Law, who was making his last football League appearance, was warmly welcomed by both sets of supporters, but little did they know what lay in store. City had also made Law their captain for the day. A loss for the Reds would almost certainly mean relegation but a draw might just be enough to stay up. The game came to life with only eight minutes remaining and the score standing at 0-0. Colin Bell and Francis Lee combined well to find Law in the United penalty area. With his back to the goal Law casually back-heeled the ball and then watched in amazement as it slipped past Stepney and into the net. Law realised what he had done and didn't even celebrate his goal as the United fans invaded the pitch. It turned out to be his last kick in League Football because when the game re-started three minutes later, Hanson had replaced Law in the game. A second invasion of the pitch and a fire in the Stretford End resulted in the referee, David Smith abandoning the game. The football League ordered the result to stand and following defeat at Stoke City on the final day of the season, United were relegated.

10. 28 APRIL 1902
The birth of Manchester United Football Club
In early 1902 Newton Heath were in serious financial trouble. They had also just finished the season in 15th place in Division Two. The club had debts totalling £2,670 and the proceeds of a fund raising bazaar were not even sufficient to keep the club afloat. However, following the meeting of creditors at New Islington Hall on 22 February 1902 at which Harry Stafford, the club's captain, informed creditors that he knew of four gentlemen who were each prepared to invest £500 in the club, the Manchester Guardian announced that The Newton Heath combination would be renamed as Manchester United. That was not the only club name suggested. Others were Manchester Central and Manchester Celtic. The name Manchester United was put forward by Louis Rocca and unanimously accepted. Mr John Henry Davies was elected the new Chairman, while Harry Stafford teamed up with the current manager, James West, to look after the day-to-day running of the new club.

THE OPPOSITION

10 CLUBS NEWTON HEATH & MANCHESTER UNITED HAVE NEVER LOST A HOME LEAGUE GAME AGAINST

1.	Accrington Stanley	P1	W0	D1	L0
2.	Brighton & Hove Albion	P4	W3	D1	L0
3.	Bristol Rovers	P1	W1	D0	L0
4.	Chesterfield	P10	W10	D0	L0
5.	Crewe Alexandria	P2	W2	D0	L0
6.	Doncaster Rovers	P4	W3	D1	L0
7.	Hull City	P8	W7	D1	L0
8.	Leyton Orient	P6	W3	D3	L0
9.	Millwall	P6	W5	D1	L0
10.	Swansea City	P8	W6	D2	L0

10 LOWER DIVISION TEAMS WHICH HAVE DEFEATED UNITED IN THE FA CUP

1.	Nottingham Forest (Div 2)	1946-47	0-2 (h)
2.	Birmingham City (Div 2)	1950-51	0-1 (a)
3.	Hull City (Div 2)	1951-52	0-2 (h)
4.	Everton (Div 2)	1952-53	1-2 (a)
5.	Norwich City (Div 3)	1958-59	0-3 (a)
6.	Middlesbrough (Div 2)	1970-71	1-2 (a)
7.	Walsall (Div 3)	1974-75	2-3 (a)
8.	Southampton (Div 2)	1976 Final	0-1 (n)
9.	Watford (Div 2)	1981-82	0-1 (a)
10.	AFC Bournemouth (Div 3)	1983-84	0-2 (a)

10 CITIES MANCHESTER UNITED HAVE PLAYED

1. Birmingham City
2. Bristol City
3. Bradford City
4. Coventry City
5. Cardiff City
6. Derry City
7. Leicester City
8. Lincoln City
8. Manchester City
10. Norwich City

10 UNITEDS MANCHESTER UNITED HAVE PLAYED

1. Cambridge United
2. Dundee United
3. Leeds United
4. Newcastle United
5. Sheffield United
6. Scunthorpe United
7. Rotherham United
8. Torquay United
9. Hereford United
10. West Ham United

10 TEAMS NEWTON HEATH AND MANCHESTER UNITED BOTH PLAYED

1. Gainsborough Town
2. Burslem Port Vale
3. Small Heath
4. Manchester City
5. Burnley
6. Barnsley
7. Leicester Fosse
8. Stockport County
8. Glossop
10. Newcastle United

10 TEAMS NEWTON HEATH PLAYED IN BOTH THE FOOTBALL LEAGUE AND THE FA CUP

1. Blackburn Rovers
2. Middlesbrough
3. Stoke
4. Derby County
5. Blackpool
6. Burnley
7. Lincoln City
8. Liverpool
9. Walsall
10. Preston North End

XIs MANCHESTER UNITED HAVE PLAYED

1. All Stars
2. Bohemians
3. Copenhagen
4. Danish FA
5. Drumcondra
6. Eire
7. Manchester United FA Cup 1977
8. Munich Combined
9. New York Select
10. Tel Aviv

10 TEAMS MANCHESTER UNITED HAVE PLAYED WITH 3 WORDS TO THEIR NAME

1. Burslem Port Vale
2. Brighton & Hove Albion
3. Bradford Park Avenue
4. Glossop North End
5. Preston North End
6. Queens Park Rangers
7. Raba Vasas ETO
8. Red Star Belgrade
9. West Bromwich Albion
10. West Ham United

10 TOWNS MANCHESTER UNITED HAVE PLAYED

1. Gainsborough
2. Grantham
3. Grimsby
4. Halifax
5. Huddersfield
6. Ipswich
7. Luton
8. Northampton
9. Swindon
10. Yeovil

THE 10 PLAYERS WHO HAVE MADE THE MOST MANCHESTER DERBY APPEARANCES FOR THE CLUB

1. Bobby Charlton — 27
2. Alex Stepney — 24
3. Bill Foulkes — 23
4. Martin Buchan — 20
5. Steve Coppell — 17
6. Sammy McIlroy — 17
7. Anthony Dunne — 16
8. Lou Macari — 16
9. Arthur Albiston — 16
10. Billy Meredith — 15
10. Roger Byrne — 15
10. Dennis Viollet — 15
10. Nobby Stiles — 15
10. George Best — 15
10. David Sadler — 15

Paul Ince of United battles with Steve McMahon of City

THE MANCHESTER DERBY

10 OCCASIONS WHEN UNITED HAVE MET MANCHESTER CITY IN A GAME OTHER THAN A LEAGUE GAME

1.	Football League Jubilee	City 2	Utd 1	20.08.38
2.	Henshaws Blind Institute Benefit	City 3	Utd 2	28.05.54
3.	FA Charity Shield	City 0	Utd 1	24.10.56
4.	FA Cup 4th Round	Utd 3	City 0	24.01.70
5.	Bill Foulkes Testimonial	Utd 0	City 3	10.11.70
6.	Alan Oakes Testimonial	City 1	Utd 3	03.05.72
7.	Tony Dunne Testimonial	Utd 1	City 2	24.10.73
8.	League Cup 3rd Round	Utd 1	City 0	09.10.74
9.	Glen Pardoe Testimonial	City 4	Utd 2	25.03.77
10.	Kevin Moran Testimonial	Utd 5	City 2	21.08.88

MANCHESTER UNITED'S FIRST 10 MANCHESTER DERBY WINS AT MAINE ROAD IN THE FOOTBALL LEAGUE

(Manchester City played at a number of Grounds before moving to Maine Road on 25 August 1923)

1.	City 0	United 1	8 February 1930
2.	City 1	United 2	31 December 1949
3.	City 1	United 2	15 September 1951
4.	City 2	United 4	2 February 1957
5.	City 1	United 3	4 March 1961
6.	City 0	United 2	10 February 1962
7.	City 1	United 2	30 September 1967
8.	City 3	United 4	5 May 1971
9.	City 1	United 3	25 September 1976
10.	City 0	United 3	10 February 1979

All games were played in English League Division 1.

NEWTON HEATH/MANCHESTER UNITED'S FIRST 10 DERBY WINS OVER MANCHESTER CITY

(Manchester City were known as Ardwick prior to changing their name)

1. Newton Heath 5   Ardwick 0   3 October 1891
2. City 2   Newton Heath 5   3 November 1894
3. Newton Heath 4   City 1   5 January 1895
4. Newton Heath 2   City 1   25 December 1896
5. City 0   Newton Heath 1   25 December 1897
6. Newton Heath 3   City 0   10 September 1898
7. City 0   United 2   10 April 1903
8. United 3   City 1   21 December 1907
9. City 1   United 2   19 September 1908
10. United 3   City 1   23 January 1909

Game 1: FA Cup 1st Qualifying Round

Games 2 and 6: Football League Division 2

Games 7 and 10: Football League Division 1

Newton Heath Football Club in 1892.

10 OCCASIONS WHEN NEWTON HEATH/MANCHESTER UNITED DEFEATED MANCHESTER CITY BY 3 OR MORE GOALS

1.	City 2 Newton Heath 5	3 November 1894
2.	Newton Heath 4 City 1	5 January 1895
3.	Newton Heath 3 City 0	10 September 1898
4.	United 4 City 1	31 August 1957
5.	United 4 City 1	14 February 1959
6.	United 5 City 1	3 December 1960
7.	City 0 United 3	10 February 1979
8.	City 0 United 3	14 September 1985
9.	United 5 City 0	10 November 1994
10.	City 0 United 3	11 February 1995

Games 1 and 3: Football League Division 2

Games 4 and 8: Football League Division 1

Games 9 and 10: FA Carling Premier League

THE FIRST 10 MANCHESTER DERBY DRAWS

1.	Newton Heath 1 City 1	5 October 1895
2.	City 0 Newton Heath 0	3 October 1896
3.	Newton Heath 1 City 1	16 October 1897
4.	United 1 City 1	25 December 1902
5.	United 1 City 1	6 April 1907
6.	City 0 United 0	18 April 1908
7.	City 1 United 1	21 January 1911
8.	City 0 United 0	2 September 1911
9.	United 0 City 0	30 December 1911
10.	United 0 City 0	5 September 1914

Games 1 and 4: Football League Division 2

Games 5 and 10: Football League Division 1

NEWTON HEATH/MANCHESTER UNITED'S FIRST 10 DERBY DEFEATS

1.	City 2 Newton Heath 1	7 December 1895
2.	City 4 Newton Heath 0	26 December 1898
3.	City 3 United 0	1 December 1906
4.	United 0 City 1	7 September 1912
5.	United 0 City 1	11 April 1914
6.	City 3 United 0	27 November 1920
7.	City 4 United 1	22 October 1921
8.	United 1 City 6	23 January 1926
9.	City 3 United 0	27 March 1926
10.	United 1 City 2	5 January 1929

Games 1 and 2: Football League Division 2

Games 3-8 and 10: Football League Division 1

Game 9: FA Cup Semi-Final (played at Bramall Lane, Sheffield)

THE ONLY 10 MANCHESTER DERBY GAMES BETWEEN NEWTON HEATH AND MANCHESTER CITY

1.	City 2 Newton Heath 5	3 November 1894
2.	Newton Heath 4 City 1	5 January 1895
3.	Newton Heath 1 City 1	5 October 1895
4.	City 2 Newton Heath 1	7 December 1895
5.	City 0 Newton Heath 0	3 October 1896
6.	Newton Heath 2 City 1	25 December 1896
7.	Newton Heath 1 City 1	16 October 1897
8.	City 0 Newton Heath 1	25 December 1897
9.	Newton Heath 3 City 0	10 September 1898
10.	City 4 Newton Heath 0	26 December 1898

(All games were played in the Football League Division 2)

THE FIRST 10 MANCHESTER UNITED v MANCHESTER CITY DERBY GAMES

1.	United 1	City 1	25 December 1902
2.	City 0	United 2	10 April 1903
3.	City 3	United 0	1 December 1906
4.	United 1	City 1	6 April 1907
5.	United 3	City 1	21 December 1907
6.	City 0	United 0	18 April 1908
7.	City 1	United 2	19 September 1908
8.	United 3	City 1	23 January 1909
9.	United 2	City 1	17 September 1910
10.	City 1	United 1	21 January 1911

Manchester City were founded as West Gorton St Marks in 1880 and in 1887 amalgamated with Gorton Athletic to become Ardwick. In 1894 Ardwick changed their name to Manchester City.

UNITED'S FIRST 10 MANCHESTER DERBY LOSSES TO MANCHESTER CITY AT OLD TRAFFORD

1.	United 0	City 1	7 September 1912
2.	United 0	City 1	11 April 1914
3.	United 1	City 6	23 January 1926
4.	United 1	City 2	5 January 1929
5.	United 1	City 3	5 October 1929
6.	United 1	City 3	7 February 1931
7.	United 0	City 5	11 February 1955
8.	United 2	City 3	15 September 1962
9.	United 1	City 3	27 March 1968
10.	United 0	City 1	8 March 1969

LEAGUE CLUBS MANCHESTER UNITED HAVE NEVER MET IN COMPETITION

1. Barnet
2. Darlington
3. Gillingham
4. Mansfield Town
5. Scarborough
6. Scunthorpe United
7. Shrewsbury Town
8. Southend United
9. Torquay United
10. Wigan Athletic
11. Wycombe Wanderers

7 LEAGUE CLUBS MANCHESTER UNITED HAVE NEVER PLAYED INCLUDING FRIENDLIES

1. Darlington
2. Gillingham
3. Mansfield Town
4. Scarborough
5. Shrewsbury Town
6. Wigan Athletic
7. Wycombe Wanderers

7 LEAGUE CLUBS MANCHESTER UNITED HAVE NEVER VISITED FOR A FIRST TEAM FIXTURE

1. Darlington
2. Gillingham
3. Mansfield Town
4. Peterborough United
5. Scarborough
6. Wigan Athletic
7. Wycombe Wanderers

LEAGUE CLUBS MANCHESTER UNITED HAVE NEVER PLAYED AT HOME

1. Barnet
2. Darlington
3. Gillingham
4. Hartlepool United
5. Hereford United
6. Mansfield Town
7. Scarborough
8. Scunthorpe United
9. Shrewsbury Town
10. Southend United
11. Torquay United
12. Wigan Athletic
13. Wycombe Wanderers

7 TEAMS WHO HAVE LOST EVERY GAME THEY HAVE PLAYED AGAINST MANCHESTER UNITED AT OLD TRAFFORD

1.	Chesterfield	10 games
2.	Loughborough Town	5
3.	Oxford United	4
4.	Rotherham United	3
5.	Crewe Alexandria	2
6.	Bristol Rovers	1
7.	Northampton Town	1

2 TEAMS MANCHESTER UNITED HAVE A 100% LEAGUE RECORD AGAINST

1.	Crewe Alexandria	4 games
2.	York City	2 games

6 TEAMS MANCHESTER UNITED HAVE NEVER DRAWN A LEAGUE GAME AGAINST

1. Crewe Alexandria
2. Leeds City
3. Nelson (no longer in the Football League)
4. New Brighton Tower
   (no longer in the Football League)
5. Oxford United
6. York City

3 CLUBS WHO HAVE DEFEATED MANCHESTER UNITED MORE TIMES THAN THEY HAVE LOST TO THEM

1.	Bolton Wanderers	38 to 36
2.	Bradford Park Avenue	9 to 8
3.	Burton Wanderers	3 to 2

Nos 2 and 3 are no longer in the Football League

8 CLUBS WHERE MANCHESTER UNITED'S VISIT RESULTED IN THE HOME TEAM'S ALL-TIME RECORD HOME ATTENDANCE

1.	AFC Bournemouth	28,799	FAC Round 6	02.03.57
2.	Hartlepool United	17,426	FAC Round 3	05.01.57
3.	Hull City	55,019	FAC Round 6	26.02.49
4.	Nottingham Forest	49,945	Division 1	28.10.67
5.	Southampton	31,044	Division 1	08.10.69
6.	Watford	34,099	FAC Round 4 Replay	03.02.69
7.	Wimbledon	30,115	FA Carling Premier League	08.05.93
8.	Wrexham	34,445	FAC Round 4	26.01.57

7 MEETINGS BETWEEN MANCHESTER UNITED AND STOKE CITY DURING THE 1971-72 SEASON

1.	United 1 Stoke City 1	League Cup 4th Round	27.10.71
2.	Stoke City 0 United 0	League Cup 4th Round Replay	08.11.71
3.	Stoke City 2 United 1	League Cup 4th Round 2nd Replay	15.11.71
4.	Stoke City 1 United 1	English League Division 1	11.12.71
5.	United 1 Stoke City 1	FA Cup 6th Round	18.03.72
6.	Stoke City 1 United 0	FA Cup 6th Round Replay	22.03.72
7.	United 3 Stoke City 0	English League Division 1	29.04.72

10 POST-WAR HOME DERBY WINS

1.	United 2 City 1	Division 1	03.09.49
2.	United 2 City 1	Division 1	31.12.55
3.	United 2 City 0	Division 1	22.09.56
4.	United 4 City 1	Division 1	31.08.57
5.	United 4 City 1	Division 1	16.02.59
6.	United 5 City 1	Division 1	31.12.60
7.	United 3 City 2	Division 1	23.09.61
8.	United 3 City 1	Division 1	05.03.77
9.	United 1 City 0	Division 1	30.09.78
10.	United 5 City 0	FA Premier League	10.11.94

10 POST-WAR DERBY DRAWS

1.	City 0 United 0	Division 1	20.09.47
2.	United 1 City 1	Division 1	07.04.48
3.	City 0 United 0	Division 1	11.09.48
4.	United 0 City 0	Division 1	22.01.49
5.	United 1 City 1	Division 1	19.01.52
6.	United 1 City 1	Division 1	03.01.53
7.	United 1 City 1	Division 1	16.01.54
8.	City 2 United 2	Division 1	28.12.57
9.	City 1 United 1	Division 1	27.09.58
10.	United 0 City 0	Division 1	06.02.60

10 OCCASIONS WHEN MANCHESTER UNITED PROVIDED THE HOME TEAM'S BIGGEST ATTENDANCE OF THE 1974-75 SEASON

1.	Sunderland	45,976	18.01.75
2.	Bolton Wanderers	38,152	08.03.75
3.	Sheffield Wednesday	35,067	07.12.74
4.	West Bromwich Albion	28,666	14.09.74
5.	Fulham	26,513	05.10.74
6.	Oldham Athletic	26,384	28.12.74
7.	Portsmouth	25,608	15.10.74
8.	Blackpool	25,370	19.10.74
9.	Hull City	23,287	23.11.74
10.	Cardiff City	22,344	31.08.74

In season 1974-75 United were in Division 2 of the Football League.

10 OF UNITED'S WORST DEFEATS

1.	0-7	v	Blackburn Rovers (a)	10.04.26
2.	0-7	v	Aston Villa (a)	27.12.30
3.	0-7	v	Wolves (a)	26.12.31
4.	0-6	v	Aston Villa (h)	14.03.14
5.	0-6	v	Huddersfield Town (h)	10.09.30
6.	0-6	v	Leicester City (a)	21.01.61
7.	0-6	v	Ipswich Town (a)	01.03.80
8.	1-7	v	Newcastle United (h)	10.09.27
9.	0-5	v	Manchester City (h)	12.02.55
10.	2-7	v	Sheffield Wednesday (h)	01.02.61

10 EVENTS IN MAY

1. 3 MAY 1993
Premiership Champions   Manchester United 3   Blackburn Rovers 1
Twenty-six years after clinching their last Championship, United were crowned FA Carling Premiership Champions after beating Blackburn Rovers 3-1 in the penultimate League game of the season. (Scorers: Giggs, Ince and Pallister.) Bryan Robson and Steve Bruce were presented with the trophy in front of a packed Old Trafford.

2. 5 MAY 1934
United almost drop into Division 3   Millwall 0   Manchester United 2
United visited Millwall on the final day of the 1933-34 season knowing that nothing short of victory would keep them in Division 2. Millwall, like United, were attempting to beat the drop into Division 3. Lincoln were already relegated and Millwall had 33 points from 41 games compared to United's 32 points from 41 games. The outcome of this game would decide who would join Lincoln. It was United's nerve that held best and they won the game with goals from Thomas Manley and John Cape. United staved off relegation to record their lowest ever League position: twentieth out of twenty-two in Division 2. United's 2-0 victory is perhaps one of the most important wins in the history of the club. Before the game the Reds changed the colour of their shirts for luck. They played in white shirts with cherry hoops.

3. 9 MAY 1953
Inaugural winners of the FA Youth Cup
Wolverhampton Wanderers 2   Manchester United 2
Having won the first leg 7-1, the Young Reds could afford to take it easy in the second leg of the Final and they drew 2-2 with Wolves' Youth Team. United's Youth Team won the first ever FA Youth Cup with an aggregate score of 9-3. Over the following four seasons United's Youth Team dominated the competition, winning the first five Finals.

4. 11 MAY 1996
The Double Double   Manchester United 1   Liverpool 0
By defeating Liverpool 1-0 in the 1996 FA Cup Final, Manchester United became the first club in the history of the game to win English football's domestic double twice. It was a remarkable achievement two years on from the club's first ever double success and reward in itself for Alex Ferguson, who during the summer of 1995 allowed Paul Ince, Andrei Kanchelskis and Mark Hughes to leave Old Trafford, and to be replaced by young players.

5. 11 MAY 1997
Joy and sadness at Old Trafford   Manchester United 2   West Ham United 0
United lift their fourth FA Carling Premier League Championship in five seasons after a 2-0 home win over West Ham United in the last game of the season. At the end of the game a unique celebration of the Reds' immense achievement was witnessed by the 55,249 strong crowd and the millions watching on television. United's four teams paraded the four Championships won by them that season: the FA Carling Premiership, the Pontins League Premier Division, the Lancashire League Division 1 and Lancashire League Division 2 titles. It was the club's first ever clean sweep of Championships.

	HOME						AWAY				
P	W	D	L	F	A		W	D	L	F	A	PTS
38	12	5	2	38	17		9	7	3	38	27	75

However, the win over West Ham United proved to be Eric Cantona's last League game for the Reds. He announced his retirement from the game during a press conference at Old Trafford on 18 May.

6.   4 MAY 1994
United clinch the Double   Manchester United 4   Chelsea 0

United, the Premier League Champions, went into this game knowing that a win would ensure their place in history by becoming only the sixth team to win English football's coveted Double. Chelsea had already defeated the Reds at home and away in the League during the season but the day belonged to United and to Eric Cantona. Cantona scored two second half penalties that along with goals from Mark Hughes and Brian McClair gave United a comfortable 4-0 victory. This victory gave United their eighth FA Cup but more importantly, the Double.

7.   5 MAY 1991
European Cup-Winners' Cup Final, Rotterdam   Manchester United 2   Barcelona 1

On their way to victory over the mighty Barcelona in the final, United won all four of their away leg ties against Pecsi Munkas (1-0), Wrexham (2-0), Montpellier (2-0) and Legia Warsaw (3-1). Mark Hughes, playing against the side that considered him to be a flop, scored both United goals. The Reds became the first English club to win both the European Cup and the European Cup-Winners' Cup.

8.   17 MAY 1969
Sir Matt Busby bids farewell   Manchester United 3   Leicester City 2

Sir Matt oversaw his final game in charge of his beloved Manchester United before he handed over the reigns to Wilf McGuinness. Best, Law and Morgan scored for the Reds.

9.   21 MAY 1977
Doc's Tigers end Liverpool's treble dream by lifting FA Cup
Manchester United 2   Liverpool 1

Liverpool, the League Champions, were out to emulate the Arsenal team of 1971 by hoping to win the Double of Championship and FA Cup success in the same season. Liverpool had also reached the Final of the European Cup. But this United team were out to prove that the previous year's defeat in the Cup Final, at the hands of Southampton, was just a blip. While Arthur Albiston was making his FA Cup debut, Liverpool's Kevin Keegan was playing his last game for the club before his move to SV Hamburg in West Germany. In the first half Liverpool played their possession game but they could not break down a United defence marshalled superbly by Martin Buchan. The game came to life in a five minute period in the second half which brought three goals. Stuart Pearson fired United into the lead only for the old 1970s cliche of, Liverpool are at their most dangerous when they are behind, to come true when Jimmy Case levelled for the Merseysiders. However, thanks to a deflected goal off Jimmy Greenhoff from Lou Macari's shot, United won the Cup. Tommy Docherty's promise to the United fans in May 1976 that United would be back at Wembley the following year to win the Cup was kept. Sadly, for many United fans, this was Tommy Docherty's last game in charge of the Reds. He was sacked six weeks later by the club over an affair that he was having with Mary Brown, the wife of the club physio Lawrie Brown.

10.   29 MAY 1968
United win European Cup Final and are crowned Champions of Europe
Manchester United 4   Benfica 1   (aet)

This became possibly the greatest night in the history of Manchester United. Ten years after the Munich air disaster Matt Busby saw his dream fulfilled when his United team were crowned Kings of Europe. 100,000 fans inside Wembley watched United beat the Champions of Portugal, Benfica, 4-1 after extra-time with goals from Charlton 2, Best and Kidd.

GOALS

10 PLAYERS WHO HAVE SCORED 30 OR MORE GOALS FOR UNITED IN A SINGLE SEASON

1.	Jack Rowley	1948-49	30 goals
2.	Jack Rowley	1951-52	30 goals
3.	Tommy Taylor	1956-57	34 goals
4.	Dennis Viollet	1959-60	32 goals
5.	Denis Law	1963-64	46 goals
6.	Denis Law	1964-65	39 goals
7.	David Herd	1965-66	33 goals
8.	Denis Law	1966-67	30 goals
9.	George Best	1967-68	32 goals
10.	Brian McClair	1987-88	31 goals

10 PLAYERS WHO HAVE SCORED 100 OR MORE LEAGUE GOALS FOR UNITED

1.	Bobby Charlton	199
2.	Jack Rowley	182
3.	Denis Law	171
4.	Dennis Viollet	159
5.	Joe Spence	158
6.	George Best	137
7.	Stan Pearson	128
8.	Mark Hughes	126
9.	David Herd	114
10.	Tommy Taylor	112

10 POST-WAR MANCHESTER UNITED PLAYERS WHO HAVE SCORED 25 OR MORE GOALS IN A SEASON FOR THE CLUB

1.	Jack Rowley	30 goals	1948-49
2.	Tommy Taylor	34 goals	1956-57
3.	Liam Whelan	26 goals	1956-57
4.	Bobby Charlton	29 goals	1958-59
5.	Dennis Viollet	32 goals	1959-60
6.	Denis Law	46 goals	1963-64
7.	David Herd	33 goals	1965-66
8.	George Best	32 goals	1967-68
9.	Brian McClair	31 goals	1987-88
10.	Eric Cantona	25 goals	1993-94

10 UNITED PLAYERS WHO HAVE A GOAL AVERAGE OF MORE THAN 1 GOAL EVERY 2 GAMES FOR THE CLUB

1.	Charlie Sagar	0.727
2.	Tommy Taylor	0.686
3.	Ronnie Burke	0.657
4.	Jack Allan	0.611
5.	Dennis Viollet	0.611
6.	Denis Law	0.587
7.	Alex Dawson	0.581
8.	Jimmy Turnbull	0.577
9.	Joe Cassidy	0.575
10.	Tom Horner	0.560

10 NEWTON HEATH PLAYERS WHO SCORED ON THEIR DEBUT FOR THE CLUB

1.	Jack Doughty	v Fleetwood Rangers (FAC) (a) on 30 October 1886
2.	George Evans	v Higher Walton (FAC) (h) on 4 October 1890
3.	Jimmy Coupar	v Blackburn Rovers (a) on 3 September 1892
4.	Bob Donaldson	v Blackburn Rovers (a) on 3 September 1892
5.	George Millar	v Lincoln City (h) on 22 December 1894
6.	Jimmy Collinson	v Lincoln City (h) on 16 November 1895
7.	Henry Boyd	v Blackpool (FAC) (a) on 20 January 1897
8.	Frank Wedge	v Leicester Fosse (a) on 20 November 1897
9.	Jimmy Bain	v Loughborough Town (h) on 16 September 1899
10.	Steve Preston	v Gainsborough Trinity (h) on 7 September 1901

10 MANCHESTER UNITED PLAYERS WHO SCORED ON THEIR DEBUT FOR THE CLUB

1.	Charlie Mitten	v Grimsby Town (h) on 31 August 1946
2.	Alex Dawson	v Burnley (h) on 22 April 1957
3.	Denis Law	v West Bromwich Albion (h) on 18 August 1962
4.	Alan Gowling	v Stoke City (a) on 30 March 1968
5.	Sammy McIlroy	v Manchester City (a) on 6 November 1971
6.	Ian Storey-Moore	v Huddersfield Town (h) on 11 March 1972
7.	Lou Macari	v West Ham United (h) on 20 January 1973
8.	Gordon Strachan	v Watford (h) on 25 August 1984
9.	Peter Barnes	v Nottingham Forest (a) on 31 August 1985
10.	Neil Webb	v Arsenal (h) on 19 August 1989

10 NEWTON HEATH/MANCHESTER UNITED PLAYERS WHO SCORED TWO OR MORE GOALS ON THEIR DEBUT FOR THE CLUB

1. William Brooks   v Loughborough Town (h) on 22 October 1898 - 2 goals
2. Jack Allan   v Burslem Port Vale (a) on 3 September 1904 - 2 goals
3. Charlie Sagar   v Bristol City (h) on 2 September 1905 - 3 goals
4. George Livingstone   v Manchester City (h) on 23 January 1909 - 2 goals
5. George Nicol   v Leicester City (h) on 11 February 1928 - 2 goals
6. Tommy Reid   v West Ham United (h) on 2 February 1929 - 2 goals
7. Tommy Taylor   v Preston North End (h) on 7 March 1953 - 2 goals
8. Bobby Charlton   v Charlton Athletic (h) on 6 October 1956 - 2 goals
9. Shay Brennan   v Sheffield Wednesday (FAC) (h) on 19 February 1958 - 2 goals
10. Paul Scholes   v Port Vale (FLC) (a) on 21 September 1994 - 2 goals

10 UNITED PLAYERS WHO SCORED ON THEIR FA CUP DEBUT FOR THE CLUB

1. Arthur Beadsworth   v Oswaldtwistle Rovers (4thQR) (h) on 13 November 1903
2. John Jack Allan   v Staple Hill (R1) (h) on 13 January 1906
3. Charlie Sagar   v Norwich City (R2) (h) on 3 February 1906
4. Bill Bainbridge   v Accrington Stanley (R3,2nd leg) (h) on 9 January 194
5. Bobby Charlton   v Birmingham City (Semi-Final) (at Hillsborough) on 23 March 1957
6. Shay Brennan   v Sheffield Wednesday (R5) (h) on 19 February 1958
7. Denis Law   v Huddersfield Town (R3) (h) on 4 March 1963
8. Lou Macari   v Plymouth Argyle (R3) (h) on 5 January 1974
9. Gordon Strachan   v AFC Bournemouth (R3) (h) on 5 January 1985
10. Keith Gillespie   v Bury (R3) (h) on 5 January 1993

10 OCCASIONS WHEN MANCHESTER UNITED'S TOP GOALSCORER IN THE LEAGUE NETTED LESS THAN 15 GOALS DURING THE SEASON

1. George Anderson   1914-15   10 goals
2. Joseph Spence and Harry Rowley   1929-30   12 goals
3. Neil Dewar   1933-34   8 goals
4. Jimmy Hanlon   1938-39   12 goals
5. Bobby Charlton   1972-73   6 goals
6. Sammy McIlroy   1973-74   6 goals
7. Lou Macari and Stuart Pearson   1975-76   13 goals
8. Jimmy Greenhoff and Steve Coppell 1978-79   11 goals
9. Joe Jordan   1979-80   13 goals
10. Frank Stapleton   1982-83   14 goals

10 PLAYERS WHO HAVE BEEN MANCHESTER UNITED'S LEADING GOALSCORER IN 2 DIFFERENT SEASONS

1.	George Wall	1906-07 and 1909-10
2.	George Anderson	1913-14 and 1914-15
3.	George Mutch	1934-35 and 1935-36
4.	Tommy Bamford	1936-37 and 1937-38
5.	Stan Pearson	1950-51 and 1952-53
6.	Tommy Taylor	1953-54 and 1955-56
7.	David Herd	1961-62 and 1965-66
8.	Gordon Hill	1976-77 and 1977-78
9.	Joe Jordan	1979-80 and 1980-81
10.	Eric Cantona	1993-94 and 1995-96

10 MANCHESTER UNITED PLAYERS WHO HAVE FINISHED THE SEASON AS THE CLUB'S LEADING GOALSCORER IN 3 OR MORE SEASONS

1.	Enoch West	1910-11, 1911-12 and 1912-13
2.	Joe Spence	1919-20, 1920-21 (joint) 1921-22, 1926-27, 1927-28, 1929-30 (joint) and 1931-32
3.	Jack Rowley	1946-47, 1947-48, 1948-49, 1949-50 and 1951-52
4.	Dennis Viollet	1954-55, 1957-58 and 1959-60
5.	Bobby Charlton	1958-59, 1960-61 and 1972-73
6.	Denis Law	1962-63, 1963-64, 1964-65 and 1966-67
7.	George Best	1967-68, 1969-70, 1970-71 and 1971-72
8.	Frank Stapleton	1981-82, 1982-83 and 1983-84
9.	Mark Hughes	1984-85, 1985-86, 1988-89, 1989-90 and 1992-93
10.	Brian McClair	1987-88, 1990-91 and 1991-92

10 OWN-GOALS BY OPPOSING TEAMS IN FA CUP AND LEAGUE CUP GAMES

1.	Bristol Rovers (h)	FA Cup 1911-12
2.	Accrington Stanley (h)	FA Cup 1945-46
3.	Oldham Athletic (h)	FA Cup 1950-51
4.	Burnley (a)	FA Cup 1953-54
5.	Derby County (h)	FA Cup 1959-60
6.	Sunderland (h)	FA Cup 1963-64
7.	Exeter City (a)	FA Cup 1968-69
8.	Ipswich Town (a)	FA Cup 1969-70
9.	Crystal Palace (h)	League Cup 1970-71
10.	Charlton Athletic (h)	League Cup 1974-75

10 NEWTON HEATH PLAYERS WHO NEVER SCORED FOR THE CLUB

1. William Booth
2. John Clements
3. William Dunn
4. Harry Erentz
5. David Fitzsimmons
6. Wilson Greenwood
7. William Higgins
8. Reginald Lawson
9. Andrew Mitchell
10. Herbert Stone

10 MORE MANCHESTER UNITED PLAYERS WHO ONLY SCORED ONE FA CUP GOAL FOR THE CLUB

1. John Aston Snr
2. John Aston Jnr
3. Clayton Blackmore
4. Garry Birtles
5. Jackie Blanchflower
6. John Fitzpatrick
7. Alex Forsyth
8. Paul Ince
9. Jimmy Nicholl
10. Mike Phelan

10 MANCHESTER UNITED PLAYERS WHO NEVER SCORED FOR THE CLUB

1. Peter Beardsley
2. Geoffrey Bent
3. Paul Bielby
4. Ronald Tudor Davies
5. Mal Donaghy
6. Darren Ferguson
7. Harold Hardman
8. Tommy Jackson
9. Jeffrey Whitefoot
10. Walter Winterbottom

10 NEWTON HEATH PLAYERS WHO ONLY SCORED ONE LEAGUE GOAL FOR THE CLUB

1. John Aitken
2. James Bain
3. William Campbell
4. James Colville
5. James Hendry
6. James Higson
7. Edward Holt
8. Charles Rothwell
9. R. Stephenson
10. James Vance

10 MANCHESTER UNITED PLAYERS WHO ONLY SCORED ONE FA CUP GOAL FOR THE CLUB

1. Duncan Edwards
2. Stewart Houston
3. Lee Martin
4. Kevin Moran
5. Remi Moses
6. Arnold Muhren
7. David Sadler
8. Harry Stafford
9. Neil Webb
10. Ray Wilkins

10 MANCHESTER UNITED PLAYERS WHO ONLY SCORED ONE LEAGUE GOAL FOR THE CLUB

1. Eddie Colman
2. Lawrie Cunningham
3. Terry Gibson
4. Don Givens
5. Graeme Hogg
6. Mark Jones
7. Chris McGrath
8. Lee Martin
9. John Sivebaek
10. Ian Ure

10 OCCASIONS WHEN A MANCHESTER UNITED PLAYER SCORED 4 GOALS IN A GAME

1.	Sandy Turnbull	v Woolwich Arsenal (h)	23.11.07
2.	Jimmy Turnbull	v Middlesbrough (h)	12.09.08
3.	Jack Picken	v Middlesbrough (h)	30.04.10
4.	Ernie Goldthorpe	v Notts County (a)	10.02.03
5.	Joe Spence	v Crystal Palace (h)	12.04.24
6.	Jimmy Hanson	v Brentford (FAC) (h)	14.01.28
7.	Joe Spence	v West Ham United (h)	01.02.30
8.	Neil Dewar	v Burnley (h)	23.09.33
9.	Tom Manley	v Port Vale (h)	08.02.36
10.	Tommy Bamford	v Chesterfield (a)	13.11.37

10 MORE OCCASIONS WHEN A MANCHESTER UNITED PLAYER SCORED 4 GOALS IN A GAME

1.	Jack Rowley	v Swansea Town (h)	04.12.37
2.	Jack Rowley	v Charlton Athletic (h)	30.08.47
3.	Jack Rowley	v Huddersfield Town (h)	08.11.47
4.	Charlie Mitten	v Aston Villa (h)	08.03.50
5.	Tommy Taylor	v Cardiff City (h)	09.10.54
6.	Dennis Viollet	v Anderlecht (ECC) (h)	26.09.56
7.	Denis Law	v Ipswich Town (a)	03.11.62
8.	Denis Law	v Stoke City (h)	07.12.63
9.	David Herd	v Sunderland (h)	26.11.66
10.	Alan Gowling	v Southampton (h)	20.02.71

10 NEWTON HEATH/MANCHESTER UNITED PLAYERS WHO SCORED 3 OR MORE HAT-TRICKS FOR THE CLUB

1.	Bob Donaldson (Newton Heath)	3
2.	Alf Farman (Newton Heath)	3
3.	Joe Cassidy (Newton Heath)	6
4.	Henry Boyd (Newton Heath)	3
5.	Jack Peddie	3
6.	Jack Picken	3
7.	Sandy Turnbull	4
8.	Jimmy Turnbull	3
9.	Joe Spence	4
10.	Tommy Reid	5

10 POST-WAR MANCHESTER UNITED PLAYERS WHO SCORED 4 OR MORE HAT-TRICKS FOR THE CLUB

1. Jack Rowley   12
2. Stan Pearson   6
3. Tommy Taylor   5
4. Dennis Viollet   9
5. Bobby Charlton   7
6. Denis Law   18
7. Alex Dawson   4
8. David Herd   6
9. George Best   4
10. Mark Hughes   4

10 HAT-TRICKS BY UNITED PLAYERS IN EUROPEAN COMPETITIONS

1. Dennis Viollet   v Anderlecht (EC) (h) on 26 September 1956
2. Tommy Taylor   v Anderlecht (EC) (h) on 26 September 1956
3. Denis Law   v Willem II Tilburg (ECWC) (h) on 15 October 1963
4. Denis Law   v Sporting Lisbon (ECWC) (h) on 26 February 1964
5. Denis Law   v Djurgardens (ICFC) (h) on 27 October 1964
6. Bobby Charlton   v Borussia Dortmund (ICFC) (a) on 11 November 1964
7. John Connelly   v HJK Helsinki (EC) (h) on 6 October 1965
8. David Herd   v ASK Vorwarts (EC) (h) on 1 December 1965
9. Denis Law   v Waterford (EC) (a) on 18 September 1968
10. Denis Law   v Waterford (EC) (h) on 2 October 1968

10 NEWTON HEATH/MANCHESTER UNITED GOALKEEPERS WHO HAD A GOALS CONCEDED AVERAGE OF 1 OR LESS GOALS AGAINST PER GAME

1. Archibald Montgomery   0.66
2. Stephen Pears   0.80
3. Robert Valentine   0.80
4. Gary Bailey   0.90
5. Chris Turner   0.96
6. Billy Behan   1.00
7. James Garvey (Newton Heath) 1.00
8. William Gyves (Newton Heath) 1.00
9. Les Sealey   1.00
10. Ian Wilkinson   1.00

BOBBY CHARLTON'S FIRST 10 GOALS FOR MANCHESTER UNITED

1.	Charlton Athletic (h) (debut)	06.10.56	Division One
2.	Charlton Athletic (h)	06.10.56	Division One
3.	Everton (h)	20.10.56	Division One
4.	Leeds United (h)	17.11.56	Division One
5.	Charlton Athletic (a)	18.02.57	Division One
6.	Charlton Athletic (a)	18.02.57	Division One
7.	Charlton Athletic (a)	18.02.57	Division One
8.	Aston Villa (h)	09.03.57	Division One
9.	Wolverhampton Wanderers (a)	30.0357	Division One
10.	Birmingham City (n)	23.03.57	FA Cup Semi-Final

DENIS LAW'S FIRST 10 GOALS FOR MANCHESTER UNITED

1.	West Bromwich Albion (h) (debut)	18.08.62	Division One
2.	Manchester City (h)	15.09.62	Division One
3.	Manchester City (h)	15.09.62	Division One
4.	Burnley (h)	22.09.62	Division One
5.	West Ham United (h)	27.10.62	Division One
6.	Ipswich Town (a)	03.11.62	Division One
7.	Ipswich Town (a)	03.11.62	Division One
8.	Ipswich Town (a)	03.11.62	Division One
9.	Ipswich Town (a)	03.11.62	Division One
10.	Wolverhampton Wanderers (a)	17.11.62	Division One

GEORGE BEST'S FIRST 10 GOALS FOR MANCHESTER UNITED

1.	Burnley (h)	28.12.64	Division One
2.	West Bromwich Albion (a)	18.01.64	Division One
3.	Barnsley (a)	15.02.64	FA Cup, R5
4.	Bolton Wanderers (h)	19.02.64	Division One
5.	Bolton Wanderers (h)	19.02.64	Division One
6.	Sunderland (h)	29.02.64	FA Cup, R6
7.	West Ham United (h)	02.09.64	Division One
8.	Everton (h)	16.09.64	Division One
9.	Chelsea (a)	30.09.64	Division One
10.	Blackburn Rovers (h)	21.11.64	Division One

MARK HUGHES' FIRST 10 GOALS FOR MANCHESTER UNITED

1.	Oxford United (a) (debut)	30.11.83	FLC, R4
2.	Leicester City (h)	10.03.84	Division One
3.	Coventry City (h)	21.04.84	Division One
4.	Coventry City (h)	21.04.84	Division One
5.	Ipswich Town (a)	07.05.84	Division One
6.	Ipswich Town (a)	07.05.84	Division One
7.	Newcastle United (h)	08.09.84	Division One
8.	Burnley (h)	26.09.84	FLC, R2
9.	Burnley (h)	26.09.84	FLC, R2
10.	Burnley (h)	26.09.84	FLC, R2

BRYAN ROBSON'S FIRST 10 GOALS FOR MANCHESTER UNITED

1.	Sunderland (a)	07.11.81	Division One
2.	Southampton (a)	05.12.81	Division One
3.	Aston Villa (h)	06.02.82	Division One
4.	West Bromwich Albion (a)	12.05.82	Division One
5.	Stoke City (h)	15.05.82	Division One
6.	Nottingham Forest (a)	01.09.82	Division One
7.	West Bromwich Albion (a)	04.09.82	Division One
8.	Everton (h)	08.09.82	Division One
9.	Stoke City (h)	09.10.82	Division One
10.	Norwich City (h)	27.11.82	Division One

ERIC CANTONA'S FIRST 10 GOALS FOR MANCHESTER UNITED

1.	Chelsea (a)	19.12.92	Premier League
2.	Sheffield Wednesday (a)	26.12.92	Premier League
3.	Coventry City (h)	28.12.92	Premier League
4.	Tottenham Hotspur (h)	09.01.93	Premier League
5.	Sheffield United (h)	06.02.93	Premier League
6.	Middlesbrough (h)	27.02.93	Premier League
7.	Manchester City (a)	20.03.93	Premier League
8.	Norwich City (a)	05.04.93	Premier League
9.	Chelsea (h)	17.04.93	Premier League
10.	Southampton (a)	28.08.93	Premier League

10 UNITED PLAYERS WHO SCORED 9 OR MORE PENALTIES FOR THE CLUB SINCE THE WAR

1.   Albert Quixall   18
2.   Steve Bruce   17
3.   Eric Cantona   17
4.   Charlie Mitten   16
5.   Gerry Daly   16
6.   Denis Law   15
7.   Roger Byrne   13
8.   George Best   11
9.   Gordon Strachan   10
10. Bobby Charlton   9

10 UNITED PLAYERS WHO SCORED 3 OR MORE PENALTIES FOR THE CLUB SINCE THE WAR

1.   Gordon Hill   9
2.   Willie Morgan   8
3.   Brian McClair   7
4.   Sammy McIlroy   6
5.   Arnold Muhren   6
6.   Peter Davenport   6
7.   Jack Rowley   5
8.   John Berry   5
9.   Denis Irwin   4 (to end of 1997-98)
10. Ted Buckle   3

10 UNITED PLAYERS WHO SCORED AGAINST A TEAM THEY LATER PLAYED FOR AFTER LEAVING OLD TRAFFORD

1.   Denis Law   v Manchester City (h)   15.11.62
2.   David Herd   v Stoke City (h)   04.09.65
3.   Brian Kidd   v Manchester City (h)   28.03.70
4.   Sammy McIlroy   v Manchester City (a)   06.11.71
5.   Gerry Daly   v Derby County (a)   24.09.75
6.   Andy Ritchie   v Leeds United (h)   24.03.79
7.   Mickey Thomas   v Leeds United (h)   08.12.79
8.   Joe Jordan   v Southampton (h)   29.11.80
9.   Garry Birtles   v Notts County (h)   31.10.81
10. Andrei Kanchelskis   v Everton (h)   11.01.92

10 UNITED PLAYERS WHO SCORED FOR UNITED AGAINST A CLUB THEY ALSO PLAYED FOR

1.	Albert Scanlon	v Newcastle United (h)	31.01.59
2.	Bobby Charlton	v Preston North End (a)	22.04.61
3.	Denis Law	v Huddersfield Town (h)	04.03.63
4.	John Connelly	v Blackburn Rovers (h)	21.11.64
5.	Stuart Pearson	v Hull City (h)	15.02.75
6.	Gordon McQueen	v Leeds United (a)	23.08.78
7.	Joe Jordan	v Bristol City (h)	23.02.80
8.	Bryan Robson	v West Bromwich Albion (a)	12.05.82
9.	Frank Stapleton	v Arsenal (h)	17.03.84
10.	Norman Whiteside	v Everton (FA Cup Final)	18.05.85

10 UNITED PLAYERS WHO SCORED FOR THE CLUB IN 5 OR MORE CONSECUTIVE SEASONS

1.	George Best	1963-64 to 1973-74	178 goals
2.	Bobby Charlton	1956-57 to 1972-73	247 goals
3.	Steve Coppell	1974-75 to 1982-83	70 goals
4.	David Herd	1961-62 to 1967-68	144 goals
5.	Mark Hughes	1988-89 to 1994-95	115 goals
6.	Denis Law	1962-63 to 1972-73	236 goals
7.	Sammy McIlroy	1971-72 to 1981-82	71 goals
8.	Lou Macari	1972-73 to 1983-84	97 goals
9.	Tommy Taylor	1952-53 to 1957-58	128 goals
10.	Norman Whiteside	1981-82 to 1987-88	67 goals

6 PLAYERS WHO SCORED FOR NEWTON HEATH IN A SINGLE GAME

(Newton Heath 10 Wolverhampton Wanderers 1, 15 October 1892)

1.	Bob Donaldson	3 goals
2.	Willie Stewart	3
3.	Adam Carson	1
4.	Alf Farman	1
5.	James Hendry	1
6.	Billy Hood	1

5 MANCHESTER UNITED PLAYERS WHO SCORED 10 GOALS OR MORE FOR THE CLUB DURING THE 1964-1965 CHAMPIONSHIP WINNING SEASON

1. Denis Law   39 goals
2. David Herd   28
3. John Connelly   20
4. Bobby Charlton   18
5. George Best   14

5 MANCHESTER UNITED PLAYERS WHO SCORED 10 OR MORE GOALS FOR THE CLUB DURING THE 1993-1994 DOUBLE WINNING SEASON

1. Eric Cantona   25 goals
2. Mark Hughes   21
3. Ryan Giggs   17
4. Lee Sharpe   11
5. Andrei Kanchelskis 10

3 TEAMS WHO HAVE DEFEATED MANCHESTER UNITED ON PENALTIES IN A CUP COMPETITION

1. Videoton   UEFA Cup   1984-85
2. Torpedo Moscow   UEFA Cup   1991-92
3. Southampton   FA Cup   1991-92

7 SUCCESSIVE LEAGUE WINS WITHOUT CONCEDING A GOAL

1. Manchester United 2 Lincoln City 0   15.10.04
2. Leicester Fosse 0 Manchester United 3   22.10.04
3. Manchester United 4 Barnsley 0   29.10.04
4. West Bromwich Albion 0 Manchester United 2   05.11.04
5. Manchester United 1 Burnley 0   12.11.04
6. Grimsby Town 0 Manchester United 1   19.11.04
7. Doncaster Rovers 0 Manchester United 1   03.12.04

5 CONSECUTIVE LEAGUE GAMES WITHOUT SCORING A GOAL

1. Leicester City 1 Manchester United 0   07.02.81
2. Manchester United 0 Tottenham Hotspur 0   17.02.81
3. Manchester City 1 Manchester United 0   21.02.81
4. Manchester United 0 Leeds United 1   28.02.81
5. Southampton 1 Manchester United 0   07.03.81

1 MANCHESTER UNITED PLAYER WHO SCORED BOTH AGAINST AND FOR THE OPPOSITION IN THE SAME GAME

1. Bryan Robson   v Sheffield Wednesday (a)   10.10.87

Manchester United won the Division 1 game 4-2

1 MANCHESTER UNITED PLAYER WHO WAS THE LEADING GOALSCORER IN THREE DIFFERENT DIVISIONS OF THE FOOTBALL LEAGUE

1.	Ted MacDougall	with Bournemouth	Division 4	1970-71
		with Bournemouth	Division 3	1971-72
		with Norwich City	Division 1	1975-76

Bournemouth were actually known as Bournemouth and Biscombe Athletic

4 NEWTON HEATH PLAYERS TO HAVE SCORED TWO GOALS EACH IN THE SAME GAME

(Newton Heath 9 Walsall Town Swifts 0, Division 2, 3 April 1895)

1. Joe Cassidy

2. Bob Donaldson

3. James Peters

4. Dick Smith

John Clarkin scored the other goal

2 PLAYERS TO SCORE FOUR GOALS AGAINST MANCHESTER UNITED AT OLD TRAFFORD

1.	Wyn Davies	for Southampton	Division 1	16.08.69
2.	Martin Peters	for Spurs	Division 1	28.10.72

7 HAT-TRICKS BY DENIS LAW DURING THE 1963-64 SEASON

1.	v Ipswich Town (a)	Division 1
2.	v Willem II Tilburg (h)	ECWC, R1 2nd leg
3.	v Tottenham Hotspur (h)	Division 1
4.	v Stoke City (h)	Division 1
5.	v Bristol Rovers (h)	FA Cup Round 4
6.	v Sporting Lisbon (h)	ECWC, Quarter-Final, 1st leg
7.	v Sunderland (h)	FA Cup, Round 6 2nd Replay

Game 4: Law scored 4 goals

Game 7: Played at Leeds Road, Huddersfield

A HAT-TRICK OF PENALTIES BY A MANCHESTER UNITED PLAYER

1. Charlie Mitten   v Aston Villa (h)   Division 1   08.03.50

Mitten scored 4 goals in the game

4 MANCHESTER UNITED PLAYERS WHO HAVE SCORED 5 OR MORE GOALS FOR THE CLUB IN A SINGLE GAME

1.	Harold Halse	6 goals	v Swindon Town (n)	25.09.11
2.	George Best	6 goals	v Northampton Town (a)	07.02.70
3.	Jack Rowley	5 goals	v Yeovil Town (h)	12.02.49
4.	Andy Cole	5 goals	v Ipswich Town (h)	04.03.95

Game 1: 1911 FA Charity Shield (at Stamford Bridge)

Games 2 and 3: FA Cup

Game 4: FA Carling Premier League

6 MANCHESTER UNITED PLAYERS WHO SCORED FOR THE CLUB AFTER THEIR 35th BIRTHDAY

Jack Warner	v Charlton Athletic (a)	36y, 139d	07.02.48
Jimmy Delaney	v Charlton Athletic (h)	36y, 13d	16.09.50
Bill Foulkes	v Real Madrid (a)	36y, 129d	15.05.68
Bobby Charlton	v Southampton (a)	35y, 171d	31.03.73
Bryan Robson	v Oldham Athletic (n)	37y, 92d	13.04.94
Steve Bruce	v Bolton Wanderers (a)	35y, 56d	25.02.96

Games 1: FA Cup, Round 5 (played at Leeds Road, Huddersfield)

Games 2, 4 and 6: English League Division One

Game 3: European Cup, Semi-Final, 2nd leg

Game 5: FA Cup, Semi-Final, Replay (played at Maine Road)

Game 6: FA Carling Premier League

6 OCCASIONS WHEN TWO NEWTON HEATH/MANCHESTER UNITED PLAYERS SCORED A HAT-TRICK IN THE SAME GAME

1.	Bob Donaldson and Willie Stewart	v Wolverhampton Wanderers (h)	15 October 1892	Division 1
2.	Bob Donaldson and Alf Farman	v Derby County (h)	31 December 1892	Division 1
3.	William Bryant and Joseph Cassidy	v Darwen (h)	24 December 1898	Division 2
4.	James Turnbull and Sandy Turnbull	v Blackburn Rovers (h)	20 February 1909	FA Cup, Round 3
5.	Tommy Taylor and Dennis Viollet	v RSC Anderlecht (h)	26 September 1956	European Cup, Preliminary Round, 2nd leg
6.	Albert Quixall and Dennis Viollet	v Burnley (h)	12 April 1961	Division 1

Game no. 5: Viollet scored 4 goals

10 EVENTS IN JUNE

1. 1 JUNE 1969
Wilf McGuinness is the new United manager
McGuinness had the unenviable task of following in the footsteps of Sir Matt and to increase the pressure on him, he was in charge of a squad of ageing players that included Bobby Charlton whom he had played alongside. McGuinness was a Busby Babe appearing in three FA Youth Cup Finals in the 1950s and also captained the England Youth team. He made his debut for United against Wolves in October 1955 aged 16. McGuinness missed the trip to Belgrade in 1958 as he was recovering from a cartilage operation and then tragedy struck again when he broke his leg during a Central League game in December 1959. He didn't play again but United rewarded his loyalty by giving him a coaching job. In April 1969, aged thirty-one, he was named by the United Board as Sir Matt's successor. To say things didn't go well for him would be an understatement and in December 1970 the United board stepped in with Sir Matt resuming temporary charge and McGuinness returning to a coaching job.

2. 2 JUNE 1894
The birth of United's first and only player-manager
Clarence George Lal Hilditch (half-back 1919-1932) was born in Hartford, Cheshire. Lal Hilditch became the first and only player-manager in the history of Manchester United after the sacking of John Chapman. Hilditch joined United from Altrincham during the First World War and played sixteen seasons for them, making a total of 322 appearances. Hilditch's appointment was always as a temporary measure and at the end of the 1926-7 season Hilditch handed over power to Herbert Bamlett but continued to play for United until he retired in 1932.

3. 8 JUNE 1990
Irwin joins United
Denis Irwin joined United from Oldham Athletic in a £625,000 transfer.

4. 9 JUNE 1981
Ron Atkinson is appointed manager
Having had a flamboyant manager in Docherty, who was then replaced with a thoughtful manager in Sexton, United decided to go for a little sparkle again in their choice as Sexton's replacement. That sparkle was in the shape of Ron Atkinson. In his playing days Big Ron was instrumental in Oxford United's rise from non-league football to Division 2. Big Ron began his managerial career at non-league Witney Town. He then moved on to Kettering Town before taking over at Cambridge United, guiding them from the depths of the Football League towards the Second Division. West Bromwich Albion tempted him away from Cambridge with the offer of First Division football and he proved a major success at the Hawthorns. Atkinson made the unfashionable West Brom side into serious Championship contenders with young players such as Bryan Robson, Remi Moses, Laurie Cunningham, Brendan Bateson and Cyrille Regis. So it was no surprise when United went after him following the sacking of Dave Sexton. At the press conference officially announcing his appointment Atkinson said 'When I was offered the job I was both thrilled and flattered, but I could not help feeling that Manchester United and Ron Atkinson were made for each other. It doesn't bother me that I was not the first choice. I prefer to think that I was offered the job in front of the best manager in the country – Brian Clough. I will not be just United's manager, I'll be an ardent fan. If the team bores me, it will be boring to the supporters who hero-worship the players. I will not allow these people to be betrayed.' Strong closing words from a man with a strong character. In his years at Old Trafford Atkinson spent heavily (£8million) but he also recouped a lot of money (£6million) with the sale of players such as Ray Wilkins and Mark Hughes.

1981-1982	3rd Place, Division 1		
1982-1983	3rd Place, Division 1	FA Cup Winners	League Cup Finalists
1983-1984	4th Place, Division 1	European Cup-Winners' Cup Semi Final	
1984-1985	4th Place, Division 1	FA Cup Winners	
1985-1986	4th Place, Division 1		

Despite the above record, which most football fans would gladly accept for their own club, it wasn't good enough for Manchester United. Atkinson was sacked in November 1986 with United languishing fourth from bottom of Division One after only one win in their opening nine league games and a 4-1 League Cup exit against Southampton. It was his failure to land the First Division Championship which undoubtedly brought his United rule to an end. Ironically it was in the League Cup where Atkinson was able to exact revenge on United following his sacking. His Sheffield Wednesday side beat United in the 1991 Final and in 1994, when he was in charge of Aston Villa, his team deprived United of the first ever domestic treble.

5. 11 JUNE 1994
Sir Bobby Charlton
Busby Babe, Bobby Charlton, received a knighthood for his long and distinguished service to football but immediately says 'I will never be able to replace Sir Matt.'

6. 14 JUNE 1970
Charlton represents his country for the last time
Bobby Charlton's England career was brought to an end when he was substituted by Alf Ramsey against West Germany in Leon, Mexico during the 1970 World Cup Finals. It was Charlton's 106th cap for his country. England lost the game 3-2 in extra time.

7. 16 JUNE 1982
Robson scores fastest goal in World Cup Finals history
Bryan Robson scored the fastest goal ever in the Finals of the World Cup when he netted against France after only 27 seconds in Bilbao, Spain. England won their group game 3-1 with Robson scoring again.

8. 23 JUNE 1988
United's Welsh dragon returns home
After what some described as an unsuccessful period at Barcelona, Sparky rejoined United. During his period at the Nou Camp, Mark had also been on loan to Bayern Munich in Germany.

9. 25 JUNE 1982
Whiteside becomes the youngest player to appear in the World Cup Finals
Less than 5 weeks after making his Manchester United debut, Norman Whiteside became the youngest player to have appeared in a game during the 1982 World Cup Finals when he helped Northern Ireland to a famous 1-0 win over host nation, Spain, in Valencia.

10. 30 JUNE 1965
Gary Andrew Pallister (defender, 1989) was born in Ramsgate, Kent.

CHAMPIONSHIP

UNITED'S FIRST 10 CHAMPIONSHIP WINNING SEASONS

1. 1907-08
2. 1910-11
3. 1951-52
4. 1955-56
5. 1956-57
6. 1964-65
7. 1966-67
8. 1992-93
9. 1993-94
10. 1995-96

10 SEASONS WHEN THE REDS FINISHED CHAMPIONSHIP RUNNERS-UP

1. 1946-47
2. 1947-48
3. 1948-49
4. 1950-51
5. 1958-59
6. 1963-64
7. 1967-68
8. 1979-80
9. 1987-88
10. 1994-95

10 SEASONS WHICH MANCHESTER UNITED SPENT IN DIVISION 2

1. 1922-23
2. 1923-24
3. 1924-25
4. 1931-32
5. 1932-33
6. 1933-34
7. 1934-35
8. 1935-36
9. 1937-38
10. 1974-75

Eric Cantona and Alex Ferguson celebrate Manchester United's second Double win in three years.

10 OCCASIONS WHEN NEWTON HEATH OR MANCHESTER UNITED FINISHED 4TH IN THE LEAGUE

1.	1897-98	Division 2
2.	1898-99	Division 2
3.	1899-00	Division 2
4.	1912-13	Division 1
5.	1922-23	Division 2
6.	1949-50	Division 1
7.	1953-54	Division 1
8.	1965-66	Division 1
9.	1983-84	Division 1
10.	1984-85	Division 1

10 CONSECUTIVE AWAY DEFEATS IN THE LEAGUE

1.	1-3	v Leeds United	26.04.30
2.	1-3	v Middlesbrough	03.09.30
3.	2-6	v Chelsea	06.09.30
4.	0-3	v Huddersfield Town	10.09.30
5.	0-3	v Sheffield Wednesday	20.09.30
6.	1-4	v Manchester City	04.10.30
7.	1-5	v West Ham United	11.10.30
8.	1-4	v Portsmouth	25.10.30
9.	4-5	v Leicester City	08.10.30
10.	1-3	v Sheffield United	22.10.30

10 WINS OUT OF 10 AT THE START OF THE 1985-86 SEASON

1.	4-0	v Aston Villa (h)
2.	1-0	v Ipswich Town (a)
3.	2-1	v Arsenal (a)
4.	2-0	v West Ham United (h)
5.	3-1	v Nottingham Forest (a)
6.	3-0	v Newcastle United (h)
7.	3-0	v Oxford United (h)
8.	3-0	v Manchester City (a)
9.	5-1	v West Bromwich Albion (a)
10.	1-0	v Southampton (h)

10 TEAMS NEWTON HEATH PLAYED IN THE FOOTBALL ALLIANCE

1. Bootle
2. Crewe Alexandria
3. Walsall Town Swifts
4. Small Heath
5. Darwen
6. Nottingham Forest
7. Walsall
8. Sheffield Wednesday
9. Grimsby Town
10. Lincoln City

10 TEAMS NEWTON HEATH PLAYED IN DIVISION ONE

1. Blackburn Rovers
2. Burnley
3. Everton
4. West Bromwich Albion
5. Wolverhampton Wanderers
6. Aston Villa
7. Preston North End
8. Accrington
9. Sunderland
10. Derby County

10 TEAMS NEWTON HEATH PLAYED IN DIVISION TWO

1. Burton Wanderers
2. Crewe Alexandria
3. Darwen
4. Woolwich Arsenal
5. Bury
6. Notts County
7. Newcastle United
8. Manchester City
9. Rotherham Town
10. Burslem Port Vale

10 TEAMS MANCHESTER UNITED PLAYED IN DIVISION ONE

1. Birmingham City
2. Tottenham Hotspur
3. Liverpool
4. West Ham United
5. Leeds United
6. Coventry City
7. Ipswich Town
8. Middlesbrough
9. Queen's Park Rangers
10. Chelsea

10 TEAMS MANCHESTER UNITED PLAYED IN DIVISION TWO

1. Millwall
2. Oxford United
3. Bristol City
4. Bristol Rovers
5. Cardiff City
6. York City
7. Fulham
8. Hull City
9. Portsmouth
10. Blackpool

10 TEAMS MANCHESTER UNITED HAVE PLAYED IN THE FA CARLING PREMIER LEAGUE

1. Swindon Town
2. Tottenham Hotspur
3. Wimbledon
4. Manchester City
5. Blackburn Rovers
6. Liverpool
7. Newcastle United
8. Crystal Palace
9. Leeds United
10. Barnsley

THE 1907-08 DIVISION 1 CHAMPIONSHIP WINNING TEAM

Henry Moger

Richard Holden

Herbert Burgess

Richard Duckworth

Charlie Roberts

Alexander Bell

Billy Meredith

James Bannister

James Turnbull

Sandy Turnbull

George Wall

Players listed are those who made the most appearances

1910-11 DIVISION 1 CHAMPIONSHIP WINNING TEAM

Henry Moger

Anthony Donnelly

George Stacey

Richard Duckworth

Charlie Roberts

Alexander Bell

Billy Meredith

Harold Halse

Enoch West

Sandy Turnbull

George Wall

Players listed are those who made the most appearances

1951-52 DIVISION 1 CHAMPIONSHIP WINNING TEAM

Reg Allen

Johnny Carey

Henry Cockburn

Allenby Chilton

Stan Pearson

Jack Rowley

John Downie

James Bond

John Berry

Thomas McNulty

Roger Byrne

Players listed are those who made the most appearances

1955-56 DIVISION 1 CHAMPIONSHIP WINNING TEAM

Ray Wood

Bill Foulkes

Roger Byrne

Mark Jones

Duncan Edwards

Jackie Blanchflower

Tommy Taylor

Dennis Viollet

John Berry

David Pegg

Eddie Colman

Players listed are those who made the most appearances

1956-57 DIVISION 1 CHAMPIONSHIP WINNING TEAM

Ray Wood

Bill Foulkes

Roger Byrne

Eddie Colman

Mark Jones

Duncan Edwards

John Berry

Liam Whelan

Tommy Taylor

Dennis Viollet

David Pegg

Players listed are those who made the most appearances

1964-65 DIVISION 1 CHAMPIONSHIP WINNING TEAM

Pat Dunne

Shay Brennan

Tony Dunne

Bill Foulkes

Nobby Stiles

John Connelly

Bobby Charlton

David Herd

Denis Law

George Best

Pat Crerand

Players listed are those who made the most appearances

1966-67 DIVISION 1 CHAMPIONSHIP WINNING TEAM

Alex Stepney

Tony Dunne

Bill Foulkes

Nobby Stiles

George Best

Denis Law

Bobby Charlton

David Herd

Pat Crerand

David Sadler

Robert Noble

Players listed are those who made the most appearances

1993-94 FA CARLING PREMIER LEAGUE CHAMPIONSHIP WINNING TEAM

Peter Schmeichel

Paul Parker

Denis Irwin

Steve Bruce

Roy Keane

Gary Pallister

Eric Cantona

Paul Ince

Andrei Kanchelskis

Mark Hughes

Ryan Giggs

Players listed are those who made the most appearances

1992-93 FA CARLING PREMIER LEAGUE CHAMPIONSHIP WINNING TEAM

Peter Schmeichel

Paul Parker

Denis Irwin

Steve Bruce

Lee Sharpe

Gary Pallister

Eric Cantona

Paul Ince

Brian McClair

Mark Hughes

Ryan Giggs

Players listed are those who made the most appearances

1995-96 FA CARLING PREMIERSHIP LEAGUE CHAMPIONSHIP WINNING TEAM

Peter Schmeichel

Gary Neville

Denis Irwin

Steve Bruce

Roy Keane

Nicky Butt

Eric Cantona

David Beckham

Andy Cole

Ryan Giggs

Gary Pallister

Lee Sharpe

Phil Neville

Players listed are those who made the most appearances

1996-97 FA CARLING PREMIER LEAGUE CHAMPIONSHIP WINNING TEAM

Peter Schmeichel

Gary Neville

Denis Irwin

David May

Ronny Johnsen

Gary Pallister

Eric Cantona

Nicky Butt

Ole Gunnar Solskjaer

David Beckham

Ryan Giggs

Players listed are those players who made the most appearances

THE FIRST 10 TEAMS NEWTON HEATH PLAYED IN THE FOOTBALL ALLIANCE

1. Sunderland Athletic
2. Bootle
3. Crewe Alexandria
4. Walsall Town Swifts
5. Birmingham St George
6. Long Eaton Rovers
7. Sheffield Wednesday
8. Darwen
9. Grimsby Town
10. Nottingham Forest

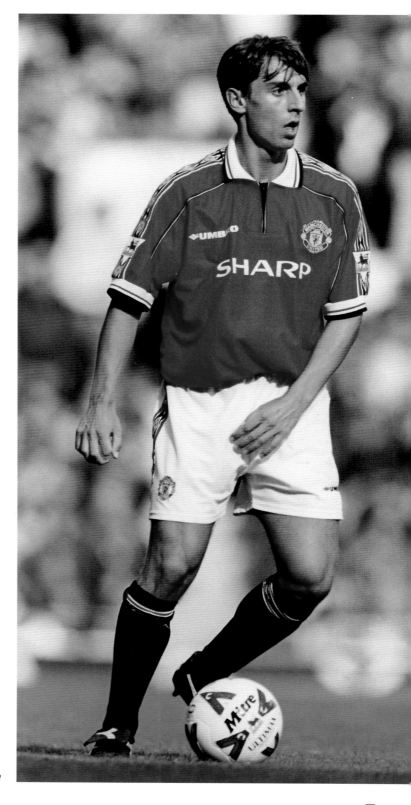

Gary Neville

THE FIRST 10 TEAMS NEWTON HEATH DEFEATED IN THE FOOTBALL ALLIANCE

1.	Sunderland Athletic	4-1
2.	Long Eaton Rovers	3-0
3.	Bootle	3-0
4.	Nottingham Forest	3-1
5.	Darwen	2-1
6.	Small Heath	9-1
7.	Birmingham St George	2-1
8.	Walsall Town Swifts	2-1
9.	Grimsby Town	3-1
10.	Crewe Alexandria	6-3

THE FIRST 10 TEAMS NEWTON HEATH PLAYED IN THE FOOTBALL LEAGUE DIVISION 1

1. Blackburn Rovers
2. Burnley
3. Everton
4. West Bromwich Albion
5. Wolverhampton Wanderers
6. Sheffield Wednesday
7. Nottingham Forest
8. Notts County
9. Aston Villa
10. Accrington

THE FIRST 10 TEAMS NEWTON HEATH PLAYED IN THE FOOTBALL LEAGUE DIVISION 2

1. Burton Wanderers
2. Crewe Alexandria
3. Leicester Fosse
4. Darwen
5. Woolwich Arsenal
6. Burton Swifts
7. Manchester City
8. Rotherham Town
9. Grimsby Town
10. Notts County

THE FIRST 10 TEAMS NEWTON HEATH DEFEATED IN THE FOOTBALL LEAGUE DIVISION 1

1.	Wolverhampton Wanderers	10-1
2.	Aston Villa	2-0
3.	Bolton Wanderers	1-0
4.	Derby County	7-1
5.	Stoke City	1-0
6.	Preston North End	2-1
7.	Burnley	3-2
8.	Sheffield Wednesday	1-0
9.	West Bromwich Albion	4-1
10.	Blackburn Rovers	5-1

THE FIRST 10 TEAMS NEWTON HEATH DEFEATED IN THE FOOTBALL LEAGUE DIVISION 2

1.	Crewe Alexandria	6-1
2.	Leicester Fosse	3-2
3.	Burton Swifts	2-1
4.	Manchester City	5-2
5.	Rotherham Town	3-2
6.	Lincoln City	3-0
7.	Port Vale	5-2
8.	Walsall Town Swifts	2-1
9.	Grimsby Town	2-0
10.	Newcastle United	5-1

THE FIRST 10 PLAYERS TO SCORE FOR NEWTON HEATH IN FOOTBALL LEAGUE DIVISION 1

1. James Coupar
2. Robert Donaldson
3. Alfred Farman
4. William Hood
5. William Stewart
6. Adam Carson
7. James Hendry
8. Thomas Fitzsimmons
9. John Peden
10. Fred Erentz

THE FIRST 10 PLAYERS TO SCORE FOR NEWTON HEATH IN FOOTBALL LEAGUE DIVISION 2

1. John Dow
2. Richard Smith
3. John Clarkin
4. John McCartney
5. Robert Donaldson
6. James McNaught
7. William Davidson
8. James Peters
9. George Millar
10. William Stewart

THE LAST PLAYERS TO PLAY A LEAGUE GAME FOR NEWTON HEATH

(v Chesterfield in Division 2 on 23 April 1902)

1. James E. Saunders
2. Harry Stafford
3. Fred C. Erentz
4. William Morgan
5. William Griffiths
6. John Banks
7. Alfred John Schofield
8. James Coupar
9. Stephen Preston
10. James Vincent Hayes
11. Hubert Henry Lappin

THE FIRST PLAYERS TO PLAY A LEAGUE GAME FOR MANCHESTER UNITED

(v Gainsborough Trinity on 6 September 1902)

1. James Whitehouse
2. Harry Stafford
3. Thomas Herbert Read
4. William Morgan
5. William Griffiths
6. Walter Cartwright
7. Charles Henry Richards
8. Ernest Dick Pegg
9. John Hope Peddie
10. William Williams
11. Daniel James Hurst

THE FIRST 10 PLAYERS TO SCORE FOR MANCHESTER UNITED

1. Charles Richards
2. Daniel Hurst
3. Stephen Preston
4. Ernest Pegg
5. Arthur Beadsworth
6. John Peddie
7. John Downie
8. Thomas Morrison
9. Hubert Lappin
10. William Griffiths

THE FIRST 10 TEAMS MANCHESTER UNITED MET IN ENGLISH LEAGUE DIVISION 2

1. Gainsborough Town
2. Burton United
3. Bristol City
4. Glossop
5. Chesterfield
6. Stockport County
7. Woolwich Arsenal
8. Lincoln City
9. Small Heath
10. Leicester Fosse

THE FIRST 10 TEAMS MANCHESTER UNITED DEFEATED IN ENGLISH LEAGUE DIVISION 2

1. Gainsborough Town   1-0
2. Burton United   1-0
3. Chesterfield   2-1
4. Woolwich Arsenal   1-0
5. Lincoln City   3-1
6. Burnley   2-0
7. Barnsley   2-1
8. Glossop   3-1
9. Leicester Fosse   5-1
10. Manchester City   2-0

Brian McClair

THE FIRST 10 TEAMS MANCHESTER UNITED DEFEATED IN ENGLISH LEAGUE DIVISION 1

1.	Bristol City	2-1
2.	Sheffield United	2-0
3.	Stoke City	2-1
4.	Birmingham	1-0
5.	Arsenal	3-1
6.	Middlesbrough	1-0
7.	Aston Villa	1-0
8.	Bolton Wanderers	1-0
9.	Blackburn Rovers	4-2
10.	Preston North End	3-0

THE LAST 10 PLAYERS TO SCORE FOR MANCHESTER UNITED IN ENGLISH LEAGUE DIVISION 2

1. Alex Forsyth
2. Willie Morgan
3. Jim McCalliog
4. Steve Coppell
5. Sammy McIlroy
6. Gerry Daly
7. Stewart Houston
8. Stuart Pearson
9. Brian Greenhoff
10. Lou Macari

10 PLAYERS WHO HAVE SCORED FOR MANCHESTER UNITED IN ENGLISH LEAGUE DIVISIONS 1 AND 2

1. William Bryant
2. Thomas Manley
3. George Mutch
4. Jack Rowley
5. Stewart Houston
6. Sammy McIlroy
7. Lou Macari
8. Willie Morgan
9. Gerry Daly
10. Brian Greenhoff

THE FIRST 10 PLAYERS TO SCORE FOR MANCHESTER UNITED IN FOOTBALL LEAGUE DIVISION 1

1. John Picken
2. Charlie Roberts
3. Alfred Schofield
4. Alexander Bell
5. John Downie
6. John Peddie
7. Richard Duckworth
8. George Wall
9. Alexander Menzies
10. Charles Sagar

THE LAST 10 PLAYERS TO SCORE FOR MANCHESTER UNITED IN ENGLISH LEAGUE DIVISION 1

1. Steve Bruce
2. Denis Irwin
3. Neil Webb
4. Clayton Blackmore
5. Paul Ince
6. Ryan Giggs
7. Andrei Kanchelskis
8. Lee Sharpe
9. Mark Hughes
10. Brian McClair

10 PLAYERS WHO SCORED FOR MANCHESTER UNITED IN ENGLISH LEAGUE DIVISION 1 AND THE FA CARLING PREMIER LEAGUE

1. Brian McClair
2. Mark Hughes
3. Lee Sharpe
4. Andrei Kanchelskis
5. Ryan Giggs
6. Paul Ince
7. Bryan Robson
8. Steve Bruce
9. Denis Irwin
10. Gary Pallister

THE FIRST 10 PLAYERS TO SCORE FOR MANCHESTER UNITED IN THE FA CARLING PREMIER LEAGUE

1. Mark Hughes
2. Denis Irwin
3. Dion Dublin
4. Ryan Giggs
5. Andrei Kanchelskis
6. Steve Bruce
7. Brian McClair
8. Paul Ince
9. Eric Cantona
10. Lee Sharpe

THE FIRST 10 PLAYERS TO SCORE AGAINST MANCHESTER UNITED IN AN FA CARLING PREMIER LEAGUE GAME

1. Brian Deane (Sheffield United)
2. Peter Beardsley (Everton)
3. Robert Warzchya (Everton)
4. Mo Johnston (Everton)
5. Chris Kiwomya (Ipswich Town)
6. Ian Drurie (Tottenham Hotspur)
7. Bernie Slaven (Middlesbrough)
8. Don Hutchinson (Liverpool)
9. Ian Rush (Liverpool)
10. Lawrie Sanchez (Wimbledon)

THE FIRST 10 TEAMS TO SCORE AGAINST MANCHESTER UNITED IN AN FA CARLING PREMIER LEAGUE GAME

1. Sheffield United (a)   15.08.92
2. Everton (h)   19.08.92
3. Ipswich Town (h)   22.08.92
4. Tottenham Hotspur (a)   19.09.92
5. Middlesbrough (a)   03.10.92
6. Liverpool (h)   18.10.92
7. Wimbledon (h)   31.10.92
8. Aston Villa (h)   07.11.92
9. Manchester City (h)   06.12.92
10. Chelsea (a)   19.12.92

THE FIRST 10 TEAMS TO SCORE A GOAL AGAINST MANCHESTER UNITED AT OLD TRAFFORD IN AN FA CARLING PREMIER LEAGUE GAME

1. Everton — 19.08.92
2. Ipswich Town — 22.08.92
3. Liverpool — 18.10.92
4. Wimbledon — 31.10.92
5. Manchester City — 06.12.92
6. Tottenham Hotspur — 09.01.93
7. Sheffield United — 06.02.93
8. Southampton — 20.02.93
9. Aston Villa — 14.03.93
10. Sheffield Wednesday — 10.04.93

FA Carling Premier League Champions 1993-94.

THE FIRST 10 TEAMS TO BEAT MANCHESTER UNITED IN AN FA CARLING PREMIER GAME

1.	Sheffield United (a)	1992-93
2.	Everton (h)	1992-93
3.	Wimbledon (h)	1992-93
4.	Aston Villa (a)	1992-93
5.	Ipswich Town (a)	1992-93
6.	Oldham Athletic (a)	1992-93
7.	Chelsea (a)	1993-94
8.	Chelsea (h)	1993-94
9.	Blackburn Rovers (a)	1993-94
10.	Wimbledon (a)	1993-94

THE FIRST 10 GAMES WHICH MANCHESTER UNITED DREW IN THE FA CARLING PREMIER LEAGUE

(All games were played in the 1992-93 season)

1.	Ipswich Town (h)	1-1
2.	Tottenham Hotspur (a)	1-1
3.	Queens Park Rangers (h)	0-0
4.	Middlesbrough (a)	1-1
5.	Liverpool (h)	2-2
6.	Blackburn Rovers (a)	0-0
7.	Chelsea (a)	1-1
8.	Sheffield Wednesday (a)	3-3
9.	Leeds United (a)	0-0
10.	Aston Villa (h)	1-1

THE FIRST 10 TEAMS MANCHESTER UNITED SCORED AGAINST IN AN FA CARLING PREMIER LEAGUE GAME

1. Sheffield United (a)
2. Ipswich Town (h)
3. Southampton (a)
4. Nottingham Forest (a)
5. Crystal Palace (h)
6. Leeds United (h)
7. Everton (a)
8. Tottenham Hotspur (a)
9. Middlesbrough (a)
10. Liverpool (h)

10 TEAMS MANCHESTER UNITED FAILED TO BEAT HOME OR AWAY DURING THEIR 1973-74 RELEGATION SEASON

1. Arsenal   1-1 (h)   and   0-3 (a)
2. Burnley   3-3 (h)   and   0-0 (a)
3. Coventry City   2-3 (h)   and   0-1 (a)
4. Derby County   0-1 (h)   and   2-2 (a)
5. Leeds United   0-2 (h)   and   0-0 (a)
6. Leicester City   1-2 (h)   and   0-1 (a)
7. Liverpool   0-0 (h)   and   0-2 (a)
8. Manchester City   0-1 (h)   and   0-0 (a)
9. Tottenham Hotspur   0-1 (h)   and   1-2 (a)
10. Wolverhampton Wanderers   0-0 (h)   and   1-2 (a)

THE FIRST 10 SEASONS WHEN UNITED ONLY LOST 1 LEAGUE GAME AT HOME

1. 1903-1904   0-2 V Preston North End
2. 1904-1905   1-2 v Bolton Wanderers
3. 1905-1906   0-3 v Leeds City
4. 1910-1911   1-2 v Middlesbrough
5. 1924-1925   0-1 v Oldham Athletic
6. 1946-1947   0-3 v Sunderland
7. 1964-1965   0-1 v Leeds United
8. 1965-1966   1-2 v Leicester City
9. 1974-1975   0-1 v Bristol City
10. 1975-1976   0-1 v Stoke City

All seasons listed above refer to Division 1 with the exception of 1974-75 when United were in Division 2.

THE FIRST 10 OCCASIONS WHEN UNITED SCORED 6 GOALS IN A LEAGUE GAME AWAY FROM OLD TRAFFORD

1. 6-1 v Newcastle United   12.10.07
2. 6-1 v Notts County   10.02.23
3. 6-2 v Wolverhampton Wanderers   01.11.47
4. 6-1 v Preston North End   30.10.48
5. 6-1 v Cardiff City   14.11.53
6. 6-5 v Chelsea   16.10.54
7. 6-3 v Chelsea   02.09.59
8. 6-0 v Blackpool   27.02.60
9. 6-1 v West Ham United   06.05.67
10. 6-2 v Everton   26.12.77

Ryan Giggs in action for the Reds during a hard-fought derby game.

2 VISITING TEAMS THAT HAVE NEVER SCORED A LEAGUE GOAL AGAINST MANCHESTER UNITED

1. Bristol Rovers
2. Doncaster Rovers

6 OCCASIONS WHEN NEWTON HEATH/MANCHESTER UNITED DEFEATED A SIDE AND THEN LOST TO THE SAME SIDE BY THE SAME SCORELINE IN A SEASON

1.	Newton Heath 7 Stoke City 1	Division 1	31.12.1892
	Stoke City 7 Newton Heath 1	Division 1	07.01.1893
2.	Woolwich Arsenal 5 Newton Heath 1	Division 2	08.01.1898
	Newton Heath 5 Woolwich Arsenal 1	Division 2	26.02.1898
3.	Manchester United 5 Newcastle Utd 1	Division 1	29.09.28
	Newcastle Utd 5 Manchester United 1	Division 1	09.02.29
4.	Everton 4 Manchester United 0	Division 1	24.08.60
	Manchester United 4 Everton 0	Division 1	31.08.60
5.	Spurs 5 Manchester United 1	Division 1	16.10.65
	Manchester United 5 Spurs 1	Division 1	18.12.65
6.	Manchester United 1 Southampton 0	Premier League	13.08.97
	Southampton 1 Manchester United 0	Premier League	19.01.98

10 EVENTS IN JULY

1. 1 JULY 1996
Eric withdraws his threat to quit

Eric Cantona withdrew his threat to quit football over the unauthorized use of his name by numerous companies attempting to cash in on his popularity. Eric went as far as taking the matter to the High Court. Eric's lawyer, Jean-Jacques Bertrand, listed British companies which he claimed had been ordered by the Court to stipulate that their product was in no way associated with Eric Cantona. Bertrand said 'Eric Cantona's lawyers will denounce and pursue anyone who uses any of his personal attributes, in any form whatever, without his authorization.'

The issue would resurface the following summer when Eric asked United for a £750,000 pay-off.

2. 4 JULY 1977
Tommy Docherty is sacked

Tommy Docherty was called before the United board after an affair with Mary Brown, the wife of the club's physio, being splashed across the newspapers. The meeting was held at the home of Louis Edwards in Alderley Edge. The directors asked Docherty for his resignation and after he refused, he was sacked.

3. 8 JULY 1991
Magnificent seven sign as trainees at Old Trafford

David Beckham, Nicky Butt, Chris Casper, Gary Neville, John O'Kane, Paul Scholes and Ben Thornley all signed trainee forms at Old Trafford. Less than five years later four of the Magnificent Seven were instrumental in United winning a historical Double Double.

4. 9 JULY 1968
Matt Busby is knighted

Matt Busby attended a service at Buckingham Palace and was given a knighthood by the Queen.

5. 12 JULY 1962
The King of the Stretford End arrives at Old Trafford

After a brief spell with Italian League side, Torino, Denis Law arrived at Old Trafford for a British record transfer fee of £115,000. It was the first time that a British club paid more than £100,000 for a player.

6. 13 JULY 1966
Old Trafford stages World Cup Finals game

Old Trafford staged the group game between Hungary and Portugal. Hungary won 3-1.

7.   14 JULY 1977
Dave Sexton replaces the Doc

Just ten days after the sacking of Tommy Docherty, Dave Sexton became the new United manager. Sexton's record before he joined United was impressive. He guided Chelsea to FA Cup success and a European Cup-Winners' Cup Final. After his time at Chelsea he moved on to Queens Park Rangers and took them to within a whisker of the First Division title. He was a quiet, considerate and articulate man. In his four years in charge of United he took them to Wembley in 1979 and FA Cup defeat at the hands of Arsenal. Sexton's United, which included players such as Gordon McQueen, Ray Wilkins, Joe Jordan and Garry Birtles, finished Division 1 runners-up in season 1979-80 but had a disastrous 1980-81 which effectively spelt the end for Sexton. He was sacked in April 1981 despite the fact that United had won their last eight consecutive league games.

8.   19 JULY 1993
Keano joins United

Alex Ferguson secured the services of a player he had admired for many years, Nottingham Forest's Roy Keane. Forest agreed to sell their prized asset after they were relegated from the Premier League. United paid Forest £3.75million.

9.   26 JULY 1966

Charlton brace puts England into World Cup Final

Bobby Charlton scored both England goals in their 2-1 World Cup semi-final win over Portugal at Wembley.

10.   30 JULY 1874

The birth of United's first great player

William Henry Billy Meredith (forward 1906-21) was born in Black Park, near Chirk, Wales.

Keane signs for United.

THE CUPS

10 CUP FINALS WON BY UNITED AT WEMBLEY

1.	FA Cup Final	1948	v Blackpool	4-2
2.	FA Cup Final	1963	v Leicester City	3-1
3.	European Cup Final	1968	v Benfica	4-1 (aet)
4.	FA Cup Final	1977	v Liverpool	2-1
5.	FA Cup Final Replay	1983	v Brighton	4-0
6.	FA Cup Final	1985	v Everton	1-0
7.	FA Cup Final Replay	1990	v Crystal Palace	1-0
8.	League Cup Final	1992	v Notts Forest	1-0
9.	FA Cup Final	1994	v Chelsea	4-0
10.	FA Cup Final	1996	v Liverpool	1-0

THE FIRST 10 FA CUP FINALS IN WHICH MANCHESTER UNITED PLAYED

1.	1909	Winners
2.	1948	Winners
3.	1957	Runners-up
4.	1958	Runners-up
5.	1963	Winners
6.	1976	Runners-up
7.	1977	Winners
8.	1979	Runners-up
9.	1983	Winners
10.	1985	Winners

THE FIRST 10 TEAMS NEWTON HEATH PLAYED IN THE FA CUP

1. Fleetwood Rangers
2. Preston North End
3. Higher Walton
4. Bootle Reserves
5. Ardwick
6. Heywood
7. South Shore
8. Blackpool
9. Blackburn Rovers
10. Middlesbrough

THE FIRST 10 TEAMS MANCHESTER UNITED PLAYED IN THE FA CUP

1. Accrington Stanley
2. Oswaldtwistle Rovers
3. Southport Central
4. Burton United
5. Liverpool
6. Everton
7. Small Heath
8. Notts County
9. Sheffield Wednesday
10. Fulham

10 TOWNS NEWTON HEATH AND MANCHESTER UNITED HAVE PLAYED IN AN FA CUP OR LEAGUE CUP GAME

1. Kettering
2. Huddersfield
3. Swindon
4. Grimsby
5. Yeovil
6. Ipswich
7. Northampton
8. Luton
9. Halifax
10. Workington

10 UNITEDS MANCHESTER UNITED HAVE PLAYED IN THE FA CUP

1. Burton
2. Newcastle
3. West Ham
4. Leeds
5. Hartlepool
6. Rotherham
7. Peterborough
8. Oxford
9. Carlisle
10. Colchester

THE FIRST 10 PLAYERS TO SCORE FOR NEWTON HEATH IN THE FA CUP

1. John Doughty
2. T. Craig
3. Alfred Farman
4. George Evans
5. Roger Doughty
6. J. Sneddon
7. Alfred Edge
8. Robert Donaldson
9. John Peden
10. Richard Smith

10 CITYS MANCHESTER UNITED HAVE PLAYED IN THE FA CUP

1. Lincoln
2. Norwich
3. Bristol
4. Coventry
5. Cardiff
6. Bradford
7. Birmingham
8. Stoke
9. Hull
10. Manchester

THE FIRST 10 PLAYERS TO SCORE FOR MANCHESTER UNITED IN THE FA CUP

1. Henry Williams
2. John Peddie
3. Charles Richards
4. Ernest Pegg
5. William Morgan
6. Arthur Beadsworth
7. John Banks
8. William Griffiths
9. Alfred Schofield
10. Thomas Arkesden

10 FA CUP SEMI-FINAL REPLAYS IN WHICH MANCHESTER UNITED HAVE PLAYED

1. 1949
2. 1958
3. 1965
4. 1970
5. 1970 (Second Replay)
6. 1979
7. 1985
8. 1990
9. 1994
10. 1995

10 ENGLISHMEN WHO HAVE WON AN FA CUP WINNERS' MEDAL WITH MANCHESTER UNITED

1. George Stacey   1909
2. James Hayes   1909
3. Richard Duckworth   1909
4. Charles Roberts   1909
5. John Aston Snr.   1948
6. Stanley Pearson   1948
7. David Gaskell   1963
8. William Foulkes   1963
9. Brian Greenhoff   1977
10. Ray Wilkins   1983

10 MORE ENGLISHMEN WHO HAVE WON AN FA CUP WINNERS' MEDAL WITH MANCHESTER UNITED

1. Harold Halse   1909
2. George Wall   1909
3. John Anderson   1948
4. Ronald Burke   1948
5. Jack Rowley   1948
6. Bobby Charlton   1963
7. Stuart Pearson   1977
8. Gordon Hill   1977
9. Gary Bailey   1983 and 1985
10. John Gidman   1985

10 IRISHMEN WHO HAVE WON AN FA CUP WINNERS' MEDAL WITH MANCHESTER UNITED

1. Johnny Carey   1948
2. Sammy McIlroy   1977
3. Jimmy Nicholl   1977
4. David McCreery   1977
5. Frank Stapleton   1983 and 1985
6. Norman Whiteside   1983 and 1985
7. Kevin Moran   1983 and 1985
8. Paul McGrath   1985
9. Denis Irwin   1994 and 1996
10. Roy Keane   1994 and 1996

10 SCOTS WHO HAVE WON AN FA CUP WINNERS' MEDAL WITH MANCHESTER UNITED

1. John Picken   1909
2. Pat Crerand   1963
3. David Herd   1963
4. Denis Law   1963
5. Arthur Albiston   1977, 1983, and 1985
6. Martin Buchan   1977
7. Lou Macari   1977
8. Gordon McQueen   1983
9. Gordon Strachan   1985
10. Brian McClair   1990 and 1994

10 PLAYERS WHO HAVE WON TWO OR MORE FA CUP WINNERS' MEDALS WITH MANCHESTER UNITED

1. Kevin Moran   1983 and 1985
2. Frank Stapleton   1983 and 1985
3. Mike Duxbury   1983 and 1985
4. Gary Bailey   1983 and 1985
5. Bryan Robson   1983, 1985 and 1990
6. Mark Hughes   1985, 1990 and 1994
7. Paul Ince   1990 and 1994
8. Steve Bruce   1990 and 1994
9. Eric Cantona   1994 and 1996
10. Peter Schmeichel   1994 and 1996

10 FAMOUS MANCHESTER UNITED PLAYERS WHO NEVER WON AN FA CUP WINNERS' MEDAL

1. George Best
2. Harry Gregg
3. Joe Jordan
4. Brian Kidd
5. Willie Morgan
6. Remi Moses
7. David Sadler
8. Nobby Stiles
9. Dennis Viollet
10. Ray Wood

10 PLAYERS WHO PLAYED IN TWO OR MORE FA CUP FINALS FOR MANCHESTER UNITED DURING THE 1970s

1. Alex Stepney   1976 and 1977
2. Brian Greenhoff   1976 and 1977
3. Martin Buchan   1976, 1977 and 1979
4. Steve Coppell   1976, 1977 and 1979
5. Sammy McIlroy   1976, 1977 and 1979
6. Lou Macari   1976, 1977 and 1979
7. Gordon Hill   1976 and 1977
8. Stuart Pearson   1976 and 1977
9. David McCreery   1976 and 1977
10. Jimmy Greenhoff   1977 and 1979

10 SUCCESSIVE FA CUP TIES WON BY MANCHESTER UNITED BETWEEN JANUARY 1994 – MARCH 1995

1.	Sheffield United (a)	3rd Round	January 1994
2.	Norwich City (a)	4th Round	January 1994
3.	Wimbledon (a)	5th Round	February 1994
4.	Charlton Athletic (h)	6th Round	March 1994
5.	Oldham Athletic (n)	Semi-Final	April 1994
6.	Chelsea (W)	Final	May 1994
7.	Sheffield United (a)	3rd Round	January 1995
8.	Wrexham (h)	4th Round	January 1995
9.	Leeds United (h)	5th Round	February 1995
10.	Queens Park Rangers (h)	6th Round	March 1995

10 NEWTON HEATH PLAYERS WHO ONLY MADE ONE FA CUP APPEARANCE FOR THE CLUB

1. Peter Blackmore
2. William Douglas
3. John Dow
4. John Earp
5. Thomas Fitzsimmons
6. Tom Hay
7. John McCartney
8. Robert Milarvie
9. Francis Pepper
10. William Smith

10 MANCHESTER UNITED PLAYERS WHO ONLY MADE ONE FA CUP APPEARANCE FOR THE CLUB

1. Peter Beardsley
2. William Berry
3. Samuel Cookson
4. Arthur Graham
5. Nikola Jovanovic
6. Neil McBain
7. Jim McCalliog
8. Henry McShane
9. John Moody
10. William Toms

10 NEWTON HEATH PLAYERS WHOSE ONLY APPEARNCE FOR THE CLUB WAS AN FA CUP TIE

1. Herbert Dale
2. J. Denman
3. John Earp
4. George Evans
5. William Gyves
6. Charlie Harrison
7. Tom Hay
8. E. Howells
9. Robert Milarvie
10. George Owen

FAMOUS UNITED TEAMS: 1909 FA CUP WINNING TEAM

Henry Moger
George Stacey
James Hayes
Richard Duckworth
Charlie Roberts
Alexander Bell
Billy Meredith
Harold Halse
James Turnbull
Sandy Turnbull
George Wall
United beat Bristol City 1-0 Scorer: S. Turnbull

1948 FA CUP WINNING TEAM

1. Jack Crompton
2. Johnny Carey
3. John Aston Snr.
4. John Anderson
5. Allenby Chilton
6. Henry Cockburn
7. Jimmy Delaney
8. John Morris
9. Jack Rowley
10. Stan Pearson
11. Charlie Mitten

United beat Blackpool 4-2
Scorers: Rowley 2, Pearson and Anderson

1963 FA CUP WINNING TEAM

David Gaskell
Tony Dunne
Noel Cantwell
Pat Crerand
Bill Foulkes
Maurice Setters
Johnny Giles
Albert Quixall
David Herd
Denis Law
Bobby Charlton
United beat Leicester City 3-1 Scorers: Herd 2 and Law

1977 FA CUP WINNING TEAM

Alex Stepney

Jimmy Nicholl

Arthur Albiston

Sammy McIlroy

Brian Greenhoff

Martin Buchan

Steve Coppell

Jimmy Greenhoff

Stuart Pearson

Lou Macari

Gordon Hill

Sub: David McCreery for Hill

United beat Liverpool 2-1

Scorers: Pearson and J. Greenhoff

1983 FA CUP WINNING TEAM

Gary Bailey

Mike Duxbury

Arthur Albiston

Ray Wilkins

Kevin Moran

Gordon McQueen

Bryan Robson

Arnold Muhren

Frank Stapleton

Norman Whiteside

Alan Davies

United beat Brighton and Hove Albion 4-0 in the Replay

Scorers: Robson 2, Muhren and Whiteside

United celebrate their 4-0 win over Brighton and Hove Albion in the 1983 FA Cup Final Replay at Wembley.

1985 FA CUP WINNING TEAM

Gary Bailey

John Gidman

Arthur Albiston

Norman Whiteside

Paul McGrath

Kevin Moran

Bryan Robson

Gordon Strachan

Mark Hughes

Frank Stapleton

Jesper Olsen

Sub: Mike Duxbury for Albiston

United beat Everton 1-0

Scorer: Whiteside

1990 FA CUP WINNING TEAM

Les Sealey

Paul Ince

Lee Martin

Steve Bruce

Mike Phelan

Gary Pallister

Bryan Robson

Neil Webb

Brian McClair

Mark Hughes

Danny Wallace

United beat Crystal Palace 1-0 in the Replay

Scorer: Martin

1994 FA CUP WINNING TEAM

Peter Schmeichel

Paul Parker

Denis Irwin

Steve Bruce

Andrei Kanchelskis (wore no.14)

Gary Pallister

Eric Cantona

Paul Ince

Roy Keane (wore no.16)

Mark Hughes

Ryan Giggs

Subs: Lee Sharpe for Irwin and Brian McClair for Kanchelskis

United beat Chelsea 4-0 and clinched the Double
Scorers: Cantona 2 pen, Hughes and McClair

1996 FA CUP WINNING TEAM

Peter Schmeichel

Phil Neville (wore no.23)

Denis Irwin

David May (wore no.12)

David Beckham (wore no.24)

Gary Pallister

Eric Cantona

Nicky Butt (wore no.19)

Andy Cole (wore no.17)

Roy Keane (wore no.16)

Ryan Giggs

Subs: Gary Neville for Beckham and Paul Scholes for Cole

United beat Liverpool 1-0 and won their second Double
Scorer: Cantona

3 MANCHESTER UNITED FA CUP WINNING TEAMS CAPTAINED BY BRYAN ROBSON

1. 1983 Replay   Manchester United 4 Brighton and Hove Albion 0
2. 1985   Manchester United 1 Everton 0
3. 1990 Replay   Manchester United 1 Crystal Palace 0

1 PLAYER WHO WON AN FA CUP WINNERS' MEDAL WITH BOTH MANCHESTER CLUBS

1. Billy Meredith   with Manchester City in 1904
   with Manchester United in 1909

3 MANCHESTER UNITED PLAYERS WHO MADE THEIR FA CUP DEBUT FOR THE CLUB IN THE FINAL

1. Arthur Albiston   versus Liverpool   1977
2. Alan Davies   versus Brighton and Hove Albion   1983
3. Les Sealey   versus Crystal Palace (Replay)   1990

3 OCCASIONS WHEN MANCHESTER UNITED SCORED 4 GOALS IN THE FA CUP FINAL

1. Manchester United 4 Blackpool 2   1948
2. Manchester United 4 Brighton and Hove Albion 0   1983 Replay
3. Manchester United 4 Chelsea 0   1994

6 PLAYERS WHO SCORED TWO OR MORE GOALS FOR MANCHESTER UNITED IN FA CUP FINALS

1. Jack Rowley   2 goals   1948
2. David Herd   2   1963
3. Bryan Robson   3   1983 Replay (2) and 1990
4. Norman Whiteside 2   1983 Replay and 1985
5. Mark Hughes   3   1990 (2) and 1994
6. Eric Cantona   3   1994 (2) and 1996

4 MANCHESTER UNITED PLAYERS WHO SCORED FOR THE CLUB IN TWO DIFFERENT FA CUP FINALS

1. Bryan Robson   1983 Replay and 1990
2. Norman Whiteside 1983 Replay and 1985
3. Mark Hughes   1990 and 1994
4. Eric Cantona   1994 and 1996

2 SETS OF BROTHERS WHO PLAYED FOR MANCHESTER UNITED IN AN FA CUP WINNING SIDE

1.	Brian and Jimmy Greenhoff	1977 v Liverpool
2.	Gary and Phil Neville	1996 v Liverpool

THE FIRST 10 OCCASIONS WHEN UNITED WERE PUT OUT OF THE FA CUP BEFORE ROUND 3

1.	1-3 v Everton (a)	Round 2	21.02.03
2.	0-1 v Fulham (h)	Round 1, 2nd Replay	23.01.05
3.	1-2 v Portsmouth (h)	Round 1, Replay	16.01.07
4.	0-2 v Burnley (a)	Round 1	15.01.10
5.	0-1 v Swindon Town (a)	Round 1	10.01.14
6.	0-1 v Sheffield Wednesday (a)	Round 1	09.01.15
7.	1-2 v Aston Villa (h)	Round 2	31.01.20
8.	1-2 v Liverpool (h)	Round 1, Replay	12.01.21
9.	1-4 v Cardiff City (h)	Round 1	07.01.22
10.	0-4 v Tottenham Hotspur (a)	Round 2	03.02.23

The Manchester United v Fulham game was played at Villa Park.

14 MEETINGS BETWEEN MANCHESTER UNITED AND LIVERPOOL IN THE FA CUP

1.	Newton Heath 0 Liverpool 0	Round 2	12.02.1898
2.	Liverpool 2 Newton Heath 1	Round 2 Replay	16.02.1898
3.	Manchester United 2 Liverpool 1	Round 1	07.02.03
4.	Liverpool 1 Manchester United 1	Round 1	08.01.21
5.	Manchester United 1 Liverpool 2	Round 1 Replay	12.01.21
6.	Manchester United 3 Liverpool 0	Round 4	24.01.48
7.	Liverpool 1 Manchester United 3	Round 4	30.01.60
8.	Manchester United 2 Liverpool 1	Final	21.05.77
9.	Liverpool 2 Manchester United 2	Semi-Final	31.03.79
10.	Liverpool 0 Manchester United 1	S-Final Replay	04.04.79
11.	Liverpool 2 Manchester United 2	Semi-Final	13.04.85
12.	Liverpool 1 Manchester United 2	S-Final Replay	17.04.85
13.	Manchester United 1 Liverpool 0	Final	11.05.96
14.	Manchester United 2 Liverpool 1	Round 4	24.01.99

THE FIRST 10 TEAMS MANCHESTER UNITED PLAYED IN THE FOOTBALL LEAGUE CUP

1. Exeter City
2. Bradford City
3. Blackpool
4. Middlesbrough
5. Wrexham
6. Burnley
7. Derby County
8. Manchester City
9. Aldershot
10. Portsmouth

MANCHESTER UNITED'S WORST 4 LEAGUE CUP RESULTS

1.	Blackpool 5 Manchester United 1	Round 2	14.09.66
2.	Manchester United 0 Everton 3	Round 5	01.12.76
3.	Manchester United 0 Spurs 3	Round 3	25.10.89
4.	Manchester United 0 York City 3	Round 2, 1st leg	20.09.95

10 OCCASIONS WHEN MANCHESTER UNITED FAILED TO BEAT A TEAM FROM A LOWER DIVISION IN A LEAGUE CUP TIE

1.	Bradford City (Div 3)	1960-61
2.	Aston Villa (Div 3)	1970-71
3.	Bristol Rovers (Div 3)	1972-73
4.	Middlesbrough (Div 2)	1973-74
5.	Watford (Div 3)	1978-79
6.	Oxford United (Div 3)	1983-84
7.	Sheffield Wednesday (Div 2)	1990-91 Final
8.	Stoke City (new Div 1)	1993-94
9.	York City (new Div 2)	1995-96
10.	Ipswich Town (new Div 1)	1997-98

Games 1-7: United were in Division 1

Games 8-10: United were in the Premier League

9 OCCASIONS WHEN MANCHESTER UNITED WERE PUT OUT OF THE LEAGUE CUP BY A SIDE FROM A LOWER DIVISION

1.	Bradford City	Division 3	1-2 (a)	1960-61
2.	Aston Villa	Division 3	1-1 (h) and 1-2 (a)	1970-71
3.	Bristol Rovers	Division 3	1-2 (h)	1972-73
4.	Middlesbrough	Division 2	0-1 (h)	1973-74
5.	Watford	Division 3	1-2 (h)	1978-79
6.	Oxford United	Division 3	1-2 (a)	1983-84
7.	Sheff. Wed.	Division 2	0-1 (W)	1990-91
8.	York City	new Division 2	0-3 (h) and 3-1 (a)	1995-96
9.	Ipswich Town	new Division 1	0-2 (a)	1997-98

Game 7 was the 1991 Final which was played at Wembley

Games 8 and 9: when the Premier League was formed in 1992-93 the old Division 2 became the new Division 1 and the old Division 3, Division 2

1992 RUMBELOWS LEAGUE CUP WINNING TEAM

Peter Schmeichel

Paul Parker

Denis Irwin

Steve Bruce

Mike Phelan

Gary Pallister

Andrei Kanchelskis

Paul Ince

Brian McClair

Mark Hughes

Ryan Giggs

Sub: Lee Sharpe for Kanchelskis

United beat Nottingham Forest 1-0 at Wembley

Scorer: McClair

3 OCCASIONS WHEN MANCHESTER UNITED MET LIVERPOOL IN THE LEAGUE CUP

1.	Liverpool 2 Manchester United 1	Final (aet)	26.03.83
2.	Liverpool 2 Manchester United 1	Round 4	26.11.85
3.	Manchester United 3 Liverpool 1	Round 3	31.10.90

4 OCCASIONS WHEN MANCHESTER UNITED MET MANCHESTER CITY IN THE LEAGUE CUP

1.	Manchester City 2 Manchester United 1	SF 1st leg	03.12.69
2.	Manchester United 2 Manchester City 2	SF 2nd leg	17.12.69
3.	Manchester United 1 Manchester City 0	Round 3	09.10.74
4.	Manchester City 4 Manchester United 0	Round 4	12.11.75

10 PLAYERS WHO PLAYED FOR MANCHESTER UNITED IN TWO WEMBLEY CUP FINALS DURING THE 1980s

1. Gary Bailey   1983 League Cup Final and 1983 FA Cup Final
2. Mike Duxbury   as above
3. Arthur Albiston   as above
4. Ray Wilkins   as above
5. Kevin Moran   as above
6. Gordon McQueen   as above
7. Arnold Muhren   as above
8. Frank Stapleton   as above
9. Norman Whiteside   as above
10. Bryan Robson   1983 FA Cup Final and 1985 FA Cup Final

10 PLAYERS WHO PLAYED IN BOTH THE 1994 LEAGUE CUP FINAL AND 1994 FA CUP FINAL FOR MANCHESTER UNITED

1. Paul Parker
2. Denis Irwin
3. Steve Bruce
4. Andrei Kanchelskis
5. Gary Pallister
6. Eric Cantona
7. Pual Ince
8. Roy Keane
9. Mark Hughes
10. Ryan Giggs

10 MANCHESTER UNITED PLAYERS WHO WON A 1992 LEAGUE CUP WINNERS' MEDAL AND A 1994 FA CUP WINNERS' MEDAL

1. Peter Schmeichel
2. Paul Parker
3. Denis Irwin
4. Steve Bruce
5. Gary Pallister
6. Paul Ince
7. Brian McClair
8. Mark Hughes
9. Ryan Giggs
10. Lee Sharpe

10 MANCHESTER UNITED PLAYERS WHO WON A 1990 FA CUP WINNERS' MEDAL AND A 1991 EUROPEAN CUP-WINNERS' CUP WINNERS' MEDAL

1. Les Sealey
2. Clayton Blackmore
3. Steve Bruce
4. Mike Phelan
5. Gary Pallister
6. Bryan Robson
7. Paul Ince
8. Brian McClair
9. Mark Hughes
10. Neil Webb

5 OCCASIONS WHEN MANCHESTER UNITED HAVE MET A MERSEYSIDE TEAM IN A CUP FINAL AT WEMBLEY

1. 1977 FA Cup Final — United beat Liverpool 2-1
2. 1983 League Cup Final — United lost 1-2 to Liverpool (aet)
3. 1985 FA Cup Final — United beat Everton 1-0
4. 1995 FA Cup Final — United lost 0-1 to Everton
5. 1996 FA Cup Final — United beat Liverpool 1-0

9 OCCASIONS WHEN MANCHESTER UNITED PLAYED THE SAME TEAM IN BOTH THE FA CUP AND THE LEAGUE CUP DURING THE SAME SEASON

1.	Middlesbrough	1969-70	League Cup R2	FAC R6
2.	Manchester City	1969-70	League Cup SF	FAC R4
3.	Stoke City	1971-72	League Cup R4	FAC R6
4.	Tottenham Hotspur	1979-80	League Cup R2	FAC R3
5.	Arsenal	1982-83	League Cup SF	FAC SF
6.	Everton	1984-85	League Cup R3	FAC Final
7.	West Ham United	1985-86	League Cup R3	FAC R5
8.	Leeds United	1991-92	League Cup SF	FAC R3
9.	Brighton and Hove Albion	1992-93	League Cup R2	FAC R4

5 CUP FINALS IN WHICH MANCHESTER UNITED WORE A WHITE KIT

1.	1957 FA Cup Final	Aston Villa 2 Manchester United 1
2.	1958 FA Cup Final	Bolton Wanderers 2 Manchester United 0
3.	1983 League Cup Final	Liverpool 2 Manchester United 1 (aet)
4.	1990 FA Cup Final	Crystal Palace 3 Manchester United 3 (aet)
5.	1991 European Cup-Winners' Cup Final	Manchester United 2 Barcelona 1

2 OCCASIONS WHEN MANCHESTER UNITED LOST A WEMBLEY CUP FINAL TO A TEAM FROM A LOWER DIVISION

1.	1976 FA Cup Final	to Southampton	Division 2
2.	1991 League Cup Final	to Sheffield Wednesday	Division 2

(United were in Division 1)

10 TOURNAMENTS IN WHICH MANCHESTER UNITED HAVE COMPETED

1.	Football League Jubilee	1938 and 1939
2.	Majorca Tournament	1962
3.	British Weeks	1966 and 1977
4.	Aberdeen Tournament	1981
5.	Europac Tournament	1982
6.	City Of Zaragoza Trophy	1982
7.	Amsterdam International Tournament	1983
8.	World Soccer Series - Australia	1984
9.	Teresa Herrera Trophy - Spain	1984
10.	Rotterdam A.D. Tournament	1984

10 CUP COMPETITIONS PARTICIPATED IN BY MANCHESTER UNITED

1. Football Association Challenge Cup
2. Football League Cup
3. European Cup
4. European Cup-Winners' Cup
5. Inter-Cities Fairs Cup
6. UEFA Cup
7. Coronation Cup
8. Anglo-Italian Cup
9. Watney Cup
10. European Super Cup

10 OTHER CUP COMPETITIONS PARTICIPATED IN BY MANCHESTER UNITED

1. Glasgow Charity Cup
2. Toronto Cup
3. Hitachi Cup
4. Adriatic Cup
5. Norwich and Norwich Charity Cup
6. British Commonwealth Cup
7. Swazispa International Challenge Cup
8. Townsend Thoresen Cup
10. Vita Cup

10 MANCHESTER UNITED PLAYERS WHO HAVE PLAYED FOR THE CLUB IN THE WATNEY CUP

1. Alex Stepney
2. Tony Dunne
3. Pat Crerand
4. Ian Ure
5. David Sadler
6. Nobby Stiles
7. George Best
8. Brian Kidd
9. Bobby Charlton
10. Denis Law

Brian Kidd

10 TEAMS NEWTON HEATH PLAYED IN THE MANCHESTER FA SENIOR CUP

1. Eccles — 1884-85
2. Gorton Villa — 1885-86
3. Ten Acres — 1886-87
4. Denton — 1887-88
5. Hooley Hill — 1888-89
6. Royton — 1889-90
7. Ardwick — 1890-91
8. Bolton Wanderers — 1891-92
9. West Manchester — 1892-93
10. Manchester City — 1896-97

10 TEAMS NEWTON HEATH PLAYED IN THE LANCASHIRE FA SENIOR CUP

1. Blackburn Olympic XI — 1883-84
2. Haydock Temperance — 1884-85
3. Lytham — 1885-86
4. Halliwell — 1889-90
5. Preston North End — 1890-91
6. Bury — 1891-92
7. Everton — 1893-94
8. Bolton Wanderers — 1894-95
9. Wigan Borough — 1897-98
10. Manchester City — 1900-01

10 TEAMS MANCHESTER UNITED PLAYED IN THE MANCHESTER FA SENIOR CUP

1. Bury — 1902-03
2. Manchester City — 1903-04
3. Stockport County — 1904-05
4. Glossop North End — 1906-07
5. Northern Nomads — 1909-10
6. Stalybridge Celtic — 1922-23
7. Crewe Alexandria — 1926-27
8. Bolton Wanderers — 1928-29
9. Manchester North End — 1931-32
10. Oldham Athletic — 1938-39

10 TEAMS MANCHESTER UNITED PLAYED IN THE LANCASHIRE FA SENIOR CUP

1. Preston North End   1902-03
2. Blackpool   1903-04
3. Bolton Wanderers   1904-05
4. Blackburn Rovers   1905-06
5. Liverpool   1906-07
6. Manchester City   1921-22
7. Rochdale   1927-28
8. Oldham Athletic   1930-31
9. Leicester City   1934-35
10. Burnley   1946-47

10 OCCASIONS WHEN NEWTON HEATH/MANCHESTER UNITED WON THE LANCASHIRE FA SENIOR CUP

1. 1897-98
2. 1912-13
3. 1913-14
4. 1919-20
5. 1928-29 (Joint)
6. 1937-38
7. 1942-43
8. 1945-46
9. 1950-51
10. 1968-69

MANCHESTER UNITED'S FIRST 10 MANCHESTER FA SENIOR CUP FINAL WINS

1. 1907-08
2. 1909-10
3. 1911-12
4. 1912-13
5. 1919-20
6. 1923-24
7. 1925-26
8. 1930-31
9. 1933-34
10. 1935-36

10 FA YOUTH CUP FINALS IN WHICH UNITED HAVE PLAYED

1.	1952-53	Winners	v Wolverhampton Wanderers 9-3 agg.
2.	1953-54	Winners	v Wolverhampton Wanderers 5-4 agg
3.	1954-55	Winners	v West Bromwich Albion 7-1 agg.
4.	1955-56	Winners	v Chesterfield 4-3 agg.
5.	1956-57	Winners	v West Ham United 8-2 agg.
6.	1963-64	Winners	v Swindon Town 5-2 agg.
7.	1981-82	Runners-up	v Watford 6-7 agg.
8.	1985-86	Runners-up	v Manchester City 1-3 agg.
9.	1991-92	Winners	v Crystal Palace 6-3 agg.
10.	1992-93	Runners-up	v Leeds United 1-4 agg.

10 PLAYERS FROM UNITED'S 1992 FA YOUTH CUP WINNING TEAM WHO WENT ON TO PLAY FOR THE UNITED FIRST TEAM

1. Kevin Pilkington
2. John O'Kane
3. Chris Casper
4. Gary Neville
5. David Beckham
6. Nicky Butt
7. Simon Davies
8. Ryan Giggs
9. Ben Thornley
10. Keith Gillespie

10 PLAYERS WHO SCORED FOR UNITED IN AN FA YOUTH CUP FINAL

1.	David Pegg	1953 and 1954
2.	Albert Scanlon	1953
3.	Liam Whelan	1953
4.	Duncan Edwards	1954 and 1955
5.	Eddie Colman	1955
6.	Bobby Charlton	1955 and 1956
7.	George Best	1964
8.	Clayton Blackmore	1982
9.	Mark Hughes	1982
10.	Norman Whiteside	1982

5 MANCHESTER UNITED PLAYERS WHO WON THREE FA YOUTH CUP FINAL WINNERS' MEDALS WITH THE CLUB

1. Eddie Colman   1953, 1954 and 1955
2. Duncan Edwards   1953, 1954 and 1955
3. Bobby Charlton   1954, 1955 and 1956
4. Wilf McGuinness   1954, 1955 and 1956
5. Anthony Hawksworth   1954, 1955 and 1956

Jesper Olsen, Gary Bailey, Kevin Moran and Norman Whiteside celebrate their victory in the 1985 FA Cup Final.

10 EVENTS IN AUGUST

1. 1 AUGUST 1990
Wilf McGuinness Testimonial
Bury 0   Manchester United 0

Wilf was at home recovering from a cartilage operation when the Munich air disaster ripped the heart out of Manchester United. In December 1959, during a Central League game versus Stoke City, Wilf broke a leg and sadly for all United fans this proved to be the end of his playing career. He was only twenty-two years old and joined the United coaching staff where he contributed to the success of the team on the field during the magical 1960s.

On 9 April 1969 Manchester United announced to the football world that Wilf had been appointed chief coach, a move made in expectation of Sir Matt's retirement at the end of the 1968-9 season. On 1 June 1969 Wilf became the tenth manager of Manchester United, but in December 1970 he was told to step down. Wilf reverted to trainer-coach of United's reserve team. Wilf moved on to manage the Greek side, Aris Salonika, and later managed York City. He spent part of 1986 on the coaching staff at Bury.

Over forty-five years after he joined United, Wilf can still be seen at the club on match days in his capacity as a member of the commercial staff. In addition to his current work at United, Wilf is very much sought after for his after dinner speaking where his wit, enthusiasm and rapport with the audience is second to none. In total Wilf pulled on the United jersey 85 times scoring 2 goals, both of which came in League games (v. Sunderland (a) on 14 April 1956 and v West Ham Utd (a) on 8 Sept. 1959).

2. 2 AUGUST 1954
Samuel Baxter McIlroy (midfielder 1971-82) was born in Belfast.

3. 5 AUGUST 1970
British soccer's first penalty shoot-out
Hull City 1   Manchester United 1

United drew 1-1 (aet) with Hull City at Hull in the semi-final of the Watney Cup and so the first ever penalty shoot-out in British soccer took place. United made it to the Final with a 5-4 win on penalties.

4. 7 AUGUST 1978
Club Celebrates 100th Anniversary
Manchester United 4   Real Madrid 0

To commemorate the 100th Anniversary of the club (as both Newton Heath and Manchester United) a special game was staged at Old Trafford between United and Spanish giants, Real Madrid. United won the game 4-0.

5. 9 AUGUST 1892
Newton Heath promoted to the Football League
Newton Heath 3   Birmingham Saint George 0

Newton Heath beat Birmingham Saint George 3-0 (scorers: Donaldson 2 and Hood) at home on the final day of the 1891-2 season to finish runners-up in the Football Alliance and thereby gain promotion to the Football League for the first time in the history of the club.

6. 13 AUGUST 1949
Old Trafford re-opened after 10 year wait

When United's first team played the reserve team at Old Trafford it was the first time that a game was played at the ground since it was bombed by the Germans on the night of 11 March 1941.

7. 18 AUGUST 1962
The King of the Stretford End makes his United League debut
Manchester United 2   West Bromwich Albion 2

Denis Law made his League debut for the Reds in front of a packed Old Trafford. Law marked his debut with a goal in a 2-2 draw with West Bromwich Albion. As a skinny sixteen-year-old, Law started his professional football career under the watchful eye of Bill Shankly, then manager of Huddersfield Town. When he was only eighteen years old Matt Busby gave him his first cap and he duly obliged with a debut goal, although it was somewhat fortunate as the goalkeeper's attempted clearance hit him on the head and ended up in the back of the net via the crossbar. In March 1960 he joined Manchester City for a British record transfer fee of £55,000 and less than a year later he moved to Torino in Italy for £100,000. It was the first time that a British player had been involved in a £100,000 transfer. Things didn't work out well for Law in Italy and in July 1962 Matt Busby had no hesitation in signing him for a British record fee of £115,000.

Over the following eleven seasons the King, as he was dubbed by the United faithful, thrilled football fans up and down the country with his tremendous aerial ability, his tenacious tackling and his goalscoring. With United Denis won an FA Cup winners' medal in 1963, scoring in the Final against Leicester City, two League Championship winners' medals (1965 and 1967) and was voted the European Footballer of the Year in 1964. Denis missed United's 1968 European Cup triumph as a result of a leg injury but more than played his part in the team's overall success in the competition. In 1973 Denis re-joined Manchester City and who could ever forget his back-heel goal for City against United at Old Trafford on 27 April 1974, a goal which helped relegate the Reds to the Second Division. At the end of the 1973-4 season Denis retired and never played competitive football again.

Appearances: FL: 305 (4), goals 171 FAC: 44 (2), goals 34 FLC: 11, goals 3 EUR: 33, goals 28 TOTAL: 393 (6) apps, 236 goals.

8. 19 AUGUST 1989
Michael Knighton takeover bid
Manchester United 4   Arsenal 1

On the opening day of the 1989-90 season Michael Knighton was introduced to the Old Trafford faithful as the new owner of Manchester United Football Club. Knighton took to the Old Trafford pitch and commenced playing keep-up with a ball. United won the game, defeating Arsenal 4-1 with new boys, Mike Phelan and Neil Webb making their debuts (scorers: Bruce, Hughes, Webb and McClair). The proposed sale of the club to Knighton fell through.

9. 24 AUGUST 1949
United Return home to Old Trafford
Manchester United 3   Bolton Wanderers 0

United played their first competitive game at Old Trafford since 26 August 1939 when they defeated Bolton Wanderers 3-0 (scorers: Mitten pen, Rowley and an own goal). League games were suspended because of the Second World War in September 1939 and Old Trafford was bombed during March 1941.

10. 28 AUGUST 1993
Record number of away victories in League
Southampton 1   Manchester United 3

United record their longest run of consecutive away victories in the League with seven wins, when they beat Southampton 3-1 (scorers: Sharpe, Cantona and Irwin) at The Dell. The victories were against Norwich City, Coventry City, Crystal Palace, and Wimbledon (last 4 away games of season 1992-3) and Norwich City, Aston Villa and Southampton (first 3 League games of season 1993-4). In between the two seasons, United also won the FA Charity Shield against Arsenal in a penalty shoot-out. However, it was still short of Tottenham Hotspur's record of ten consecutive away victories which they set during their 1960-61 Double winning season.

EUROPE

THE FIRST 10 TEAMS MANCHESTER UNITED PLAYED IN THE EUROPEAN CUP

1.	RSC Anderlecht	1956-57
2.	Borussia Dortmund	1956-57
3.	Athletic Bilbao	1956-57
4.	Real Madrid	1956-57
5.	Shamrock Rovers	1957-58
6.	Dukla Prague	1957-58
7.	Red Star Belgrade	1957-58
8.	AC Milan	1957-58
9.	HJK Helsinki	1965-66
10.	ASK Vorwarts	1965-66

THE FIRST 10 PLAYERS WHO HAVE SCORED FOR MANCHESTER UNITED IN A EUROPEAN CUP TIE

1.	Dennis Viollet	1956-57
2.	Tommy Taylor	1956-57
3.	Liam Whelan	1956-57
4.	Johnny Berry	1956-57
5.	David Pegg	1956-57
6.	Bobby Charlton	1956-57
7.	Colin Webster	1957-58
8.	Eddie Colman	1957-58
9.	John Connelly	1965-66
10.	David Herd	1965-66

THE FIRST 10 TEAMS MANCHESTER UNITED PLAYED IN A EUROPEAN CUP-WINNERS' CUP TIE

1.	Willem II	1963-64
2.	Tottenham Hotspur	1963-64
3.	Sporting Club Lisbon	1963-64
4.	AS Saint-Etienne	1977-78
5.	FC Porto	1977-78
6.	Dukla Prague	1983-84
7.	Spartak Varna	1983-84
8.	FC Barcelona	1983-84
9.	Juventus	1983-84
10.	Pecsi Munkas	1990-91

THE FIRST 10 TEAMS MANCHESTER UNITED PLAYED IN THE INTER-CITIES FAIRS CUP OR UEFA CUP

1.	Djurgardens IF	1964-65
2.	Borussia Dortmund	1964-65
3.	Everton	1964-65
4.	RC Strasbourg	1964-65
5.	Ferencvaros	1964-65
6.	Ajax Amsterdam	1976-77
7.	Juventus	1976-77
8.	Widzew Lodz	1980-81
9.	Valencia	1980-81
10.	Raba Vasas ETO	1984-85

THE FIRST 10 PLAYERS WHO SCORED FOR MANCHESTER UNITED IN THE INTER-CITIES FAIRS CUP OR UEFA CUP

1.	David Herd	ICFC	1964-65
2.	Denis Law	ICFC	1964-65
3.	Bobby Charlton	ICFC	1964-65
4.	George Best	ICFC	1964-65
5.	John Connelly	ICFC	1964-65
6.	Sammy McIlroy	UEFA Cup	1976-77
7.	Lou Macari	UEFA Cup	1976-77
8.	Gordon Hill	UEFA Cup	1976-77
9.	Bryan Robson	UEFA Cup	1982-83
10.	Arnold Muhren	UEFA Cup	1982-83

10 ENGLISHMEN WHO WON A EUROPEAN CUP-WINNERS' CUP WINNERS' MEDAL WITH MANCHESTER UNITED IN 1991

1. Les Sealey
2. Steve Bruce
3. Mike Phelan
4. Gary Pallister
5. Bryan Robson
6. Paul Ince
7. Lee Sharpe
8. Neil Webb
9. Mark Robins
10. Danny Wallace

10 MANCHESTER UNITED PLAYERS WHO NEVER WON A EUROPEAN WINNERS' MEDAL WITH THE CLUB

1. Denis Law
2. Martin Buchan
3. Lou Macari
4. Kevin Moran
5. Frank Stapleton
6. Noel Cantwell
7. Johnny Carey
8. Harry Gregg
9. Gary Bailey
10. Steve Coppell

THE FIRST 10 PLAYERS TO SCORE FOR MANCHESTER UNITED IN THE EUROPEAN CUP-WINNERS' CUP

1. David Herd
2. Denis Law
3. Bobby Charlton
4. John Chisnall
5. Maurice Setters
6. Gordon Hill
7. Steve Coppell
8. Stuart Pearson
9. Jimmy Nicholl
10. Ray Wilkins

10 PLAYERS WHO HAVE SCORED FOR MANCHESTER UNITED IN TWO OR MORE DIFFERENT EUROPEAN COMPETITIONS

1. Bobby Charlton   EC, ICFC and ECWC
2. Denis Law   EC, ICFC and ECWC
3. David Herd   EC, ICFC and ECWC
4. George Best   EC and ICFC
5. John Connelly   EC and ICFC
6. Gordon Hill   UEFA Cup and ECWC
7. Bryan Robson   EC, UEFA Cup and ECWC
8. Frank Stapleton   UEFA Cup and ECWC
9. Mark Hughes   EC, UEFA Cup and ECWC
10. Steve Bruce   EC and ECWC

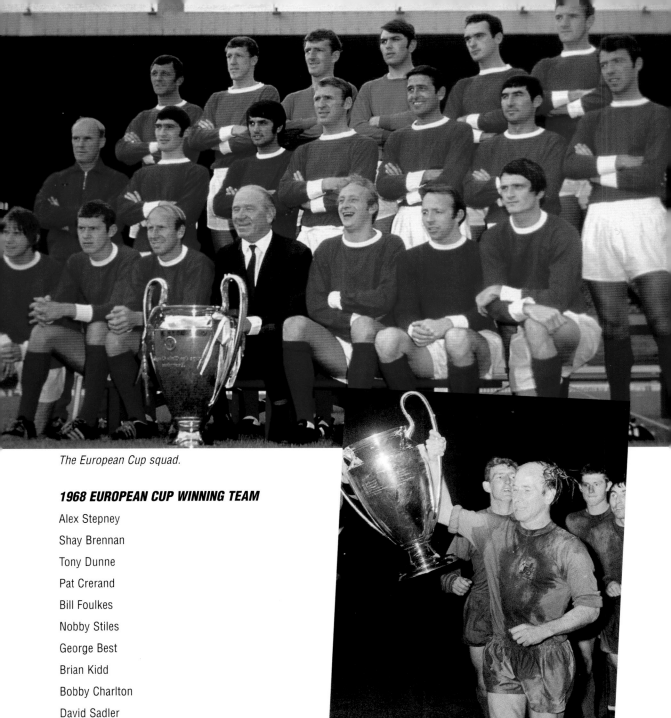

The European Cup squad.

1968 EUROPEAN CUP WINNING TEAM

Alex Stepney

Shay Brennan

Tony Dunne

Pat Crerand

Bill Foulkes

Nobby Stiles

George Best

Brian Kidd

Bobby Charlton

David Sadler

John Aston Jnr.

United beat Benfica (Portugal) 4-1 after extra time at Wembley Stadium

Scorers: Charlton 2, Best and Kidd

Bobby Charlton carries the European Cup around Wembley.

THE FIRST 10 DEFEATS MANCHESTER UNITED SUFFERED IN A EUROPEAN CUP GAME

(All 10 defeats were encountered in the Away leg)

1.	Athletico Bilbao	3-5	1956-57
2.	Real Madrid	1-3	1956-57
3.	Dukla Prague	0-1	1957-58
4.	AC Milan	0-4	1957-58
5.	FK Partizan Belgrade	0-2	1965-66
6.	Gornik Zagreb	0-1	1967-68
7.	RSC Anderlecht	1-3	1968-69
8.	AC Milan	0-2	1968-69
9.	Barcelona	0-4	1993-94*
10.	IFK Gothenburg	1-3	1993-94*

*The European Cup was known as The UEFA Champions League

1991 EUROPEAN CUP-WINNERS' CUP WINNING TEAM

Les Sealey

Denis Irwin

Clayton Blackmore

Steve Bruce

Mike Phelan

Gary Pallister

Bryan Robson

Paul Ince

Brian McClair

Mark Hughes

Lee Sharpe

United beat Barcelona (Spain) 2-1 in Rotterdam, Holland

Scorer: Hughes 2

1991 EUROPEAN SUPER CUP WINNING TEAM

Peter Schmeichel

Denis Irwin

Lee Martin

Steve Bruce

Neil Webb

Gary Pallister

Andrei Kanchelskis

Paul Ince

Brian McClair

Mark Hughes

Clayton Blackmore

Sub: Ryan Giggs for Martin

United beat Red Star Belgrade (Yugoslavia) 1-0 at Old Trafford

Scorer: McClair

1968 WORLD CLUB CHAMPIONSHIP SQUAD

1.	Alex Stepney	(h and a legs)
2.	Tony Dunne	(h and a legs)
3.	Francis Burns	(h leg)
4.	Shay Brennan	(a leg)
5.	Pat Crerand	(h and a legs)
6.	Bill Foulkes	(h and a legs)
7.	Nobby Stiles	(h leg)
8.	Willie Morgan	(h and a legs)
9.	David Sadler	(h and a legs)
10.	Bobby Charlton	(h and a legs)
11.	Denis Law	(h and a legs)
12.	George Best	(h and a legs)

Sub: Carlo Sartori for Law in away leg

United lost 0-1 to Estudiantes de la Plata (Argentina) in the away leg and drew 1-1 at Old Trafford. United lost 1-2 on aggregate.

Scorer: Morgan

UNITED'S 10 LEADING GOALSCORERS IN EUROPEAN COMPETITION

1.	Denis Law	28 goals
2.	Bobby Charlton	22
3.	David Herd	14
4.	Dennis Viollet	13
5.	George Best	11
6.	John Connelly	11
7.	Tommy Taylor	11
8.	Mark Hughes	9
9.	Bryan Robson	8
10.	Andy Cole (to end of season 1997-98)	6

10 COUNTRIES WHERE MANCHESTER UNITED HAVE NEVER LOST A EUROPEAN TIE

(Statistics are up to the end of season 1997-98)

1. Austria
2. Bulgaria
3. East Germany
4. Eire
5. Finland
6. France
7. Greece
8. Malta
9. Russia
10. Scotland

10 COUNTRIES WHERE MANCHESTER UNITED HAVE PLAYED A EUROPEAN CUP TIE

1. Belgium   RSC Anderlecht
2. West Germany   Borussia Dortmund
3. Spain   Real Madrid
4. Republic of Ireland (Eire)   Waterford
5. Czechoslovakia   Dukla Prague
6. Yugoslavia   Red Star Belgrade
7. Italy   AC Milan
8. Finland   HJK Helsinki
9. Portugal   Benfica
10. Malta   Hibernians

10 COUNTRIES WHERE MANCHESTER UNITED HAVE PLAYED A EUROPEAN CUP-WINNERS' CUP TIE

1. Holland   Willem II
2. England   Tottenham Hotspur
3. Portugal   Sporting Club Lisbon
4. France   AS Saint-Etienne
5. Czechoslovakia   Dukla Prague
6. Spain   FC Barcelona
7. Italy   Juventus
8. Hungary   Pecsi Munkas
9. Wales   Wrexham
10. Poland   Legia Warsaw

10 COUNTRIES WHERE MANCHESTER UNITED HAVE PLAYED AN INTER-CITIES FAIRS CUP OR UEFA CUP TIE

1. West Germany   Borussia Dortmund
2. England   Everton
3. France   RC Strasbourg
4. Hungary   Ferencvaros
5. Holland   Ajax Amsterdam
6. Italy   Juventus
7. Poland   Widzew Lodz
8. Spain   Valencia CF
9. Scotland   Dundee United
10. Russia   Torpedo Moscow

3 MANCHESTER UNITED PLAYERS WHO WON THE EUROPEAN FOOTBALLER OF THE YEAR AWARD

1. Denis Law   1964
2. Bobby Charlton   1966
3. George Best   1968

6 ENGLISH LEAGUE GROUNDS ON WHICH MANCHESTER UNITED HAVE PLAYED A EUROPEAN TIE

1. Maine Road (used by United for European Cup games after Old Trafford was bombed during World War II)
2. Old Trafford
3. White Hart Lane (v Spurs in the 1963-64 European Cup-Winners' Cup)
4. Goodison Park (v Everton in the 1964-65 Inter-Cities Fairs Cup)
5. Home Park, Plymouth (v AS Saint Etienne in the 1977-78 European Cup-Winners' Cup)
6. The Racecourse Ground (v Wrexham in the 1990-91 European Cup-Winners' Cup)

2 MANAGERS WHO WON EUROPEAN TROPHIES FOR MANCHESTER UNITED

1.	Matt Busby	European Cup	1968
2.	Alex Ferguson	European Cup-Winners' Cup	1991
		European Super Cup	1991

11 TEAMS MANCHESTER UNITED HAVE MET THREE TIMES IN EUROPEAN COMPETITION

1. AC Milan
2. Anderlecht
3. Benfica
4. Borussia Dortmund
5. Dukla Prague
6. Galatasaray
7. Rapid Vienna
8. Real Madrid
9. FC Barcelona
10. Red Star Belgrade
11. Juventus

10 EVENTS IN SEPTEMBER

1.   2 SEPTEMBER 1893
Peden becomes first Irish Heathen as club gets a new home
Newton Heath 3   Burnley 2

At the end of the 1892-3 season Newton Heath moved from its North Road Ground to a new home at Bank Street, Clayton. A crowd of 10,000 turned up to witness a 3-2 win over Burnley thanks to an Alfred Farman hat-trick. Jack Peden made his debut for the Heathens and became the first Irish player to play league football for the club.
PEDEN, Jack (Forward 1893-1894) - debut in above game.
Appearances: FL: 28, goals 7 FAC: 3, goals 1 TM: 1, goals 0
TOTAL: 32 apps, 8 goals.

2.   3 SEPTEMBER 1892
Defeat for Heathens in their first football League game
Blackburn Rovers 4   Newton Heath 3

Newton Heath lose their first ever game in the Football League, going down 4-3 at Blackburn Rovers.

3.   3 SEPTEMBER 1983
1,000th victory in Division One
Stoke City 0   Manchester United 1

Arnold Muhren scored the goal which gave the Reds their 1,000th victory in Division One. The wins were achieved against fifty-one different teams.

4.   6 SEPTEMBER 1902
Manchester United's first ever League game
Gainsborough Trinity 0   Manchester United 1

Following the bankruptcy of Newton Heath, Manchester United played their first ever League game under their new name. Chas Richards had the honour of scoring the first ever goal for Manchester United.

5.   8 SEPTEMBER 1894
Longest ever run of away defeats
Burton 1   Newton Heath 0

The club's longest ever run of away defeats in all competitions is set when the Heathens lose their fifteenth consecutive game, 1-0 at Burton on the opening day of the 1894-5 season. The losing sequence began back on 30 September 1893 with a 1-0 reversal at Darwen. Unbelievably the defeat was also their twenty-fifth loss away from home in their previous 26 games!

6.   12 SEPTEMBER 1956
United defy the FA to pioneer Europe
RSC Anderlecht 0   Manchester United 2

United defied football League orders and participated in their first ever European fixture. Stanley Rous, secretary of the Football Association, finally gave the Reds the go ahead to compete. United played Anderlecht in Belgium in the preliminary round (first leg) of the European Cup. United won the game 2-0 with goals from Viollet and Taylor in front of 35,000 people.

The United team on this historic occasion was: Wood, Foulkes, Byrne, Colman, Jones, Blanchflower, Berry, Whelan, Taylor, Viollet, Pegg

7.   14 SEPTEMBER 1963
Best of the Best
Manchester United 1   West Bromwich Albion 0

This game will live forever in the memory of 50,453 people lucky enough to have been present because they witnessed the League debut of a young, skinny Irishman by the name of George Best. The first real football superstar, George Best had everything a young man could possibly want: unbelievable talent, good looks and wealth. On the field 'the fifth Beatle', as he became known, entertained alongside two other United legends: Bobby Charlton and Denis Law. George helped the Reds to two First Division Championships in 1964-5 and 1966-7 and to European Cup success in 1968. He played for United for 11 seasons (1963-74) and was the Reds' leading goalscorer in the League for five consecutive seasons (1967-8 to 1971-2). Despite his acrimonious departure from Old Trafford and the odd bit of trouble he got himself into after Sir Matt Busby retired, George for many was the Greatest Player in the World, something which even the great Pele once conceded.
Appearances: FL: 361, goals 137 FAC: 46, goals 21 FLC: 25, goals 9
EUR: 34, goals 11 TOTAL: 466 apps, 178 goals.

8.   21 SEPTEMBER 1889
Club play first ever game in Football Alliance
Newton Heath 4   Sunderland 1

Newton Heath played their first ever game in the Football Alliance and beat Sunderland 4-1 (scorers: Wilson 2, Doughty J and Stewart). The game also marked the first time that a pair of brothers played for the club in the same side when Jack and Roger Doughty took to the field.

9.   25 SEPTEMBER 1937
Johnny Carey makes his United debut
Manchester United 1   Southampton 2

Johnny Carey was signed for United by A. Scott Duncan in 1935 from St James' Gate for £250. On the field of play Carey was a tough but very accomplished and stylish defender who never shirked a tackle. Off the field, he was a quiet, private person. Johnny played in 10 different positions for the Reds, including goalkeeper, making 306 league appearances. At international level, he played for both Northern Ireland (seven caps) and the Republic of Ireland (twenty-nine caps). In September 1946 he set a record of playing against England twice in the space of only three days for both Irish sides. Carey led United to FA Cup success over Blackpool in the 1948 Final and was a member of the side which clinched a first League title for Matt Busby in season 1951-2. He captained the Republic of Ireland to a famous win over England at Goodison Park, Liverpool to become the first side ever to win on English soil against the national side. In 1947 he captained the Rest of the World team which played a Great Britain side at Hampden Park to mark the Football Association's re-entry into FIFA. In 1949 he won the prestigious Footballer of the Year Award. Carey retired in 1953 and sadly he died at the age of 76 in August 1995.

10.   26 SEPTEMBER 1956
United's record score
Manchester United 10   RSC Anderlecht 0

United play their first ever European tie, (played at Maine Road), defeating Anderlecht 10-0 in the second leg of their European Cup preliminary round encounter. The 10-0 (scorers: Viollet 4, Taylor 3, Whelan 2 and Berry) scoreline remains United's record scoreline in European competition. The game marked the first ever competitive European tie to be played in England. With the 2-0 away leg win, the aggregate score of 12-0 is an all time record for the club.

INTERNATIONALS

THE FIRST 10 MANCHESTER UNITED PLAYERS CAPPED AT INTERNATIONAL LEVEL BY ENGLAND

1. Charles Roberts   1905
2. George Wall   1907
3. Harold Halse   1909
4. John Mew   1920
5. John Silcock   1921
6. Joseph Spence   1926
7. Henry Cockburn   1946
8. John Aston Snr.   1948
9. Stanley Pearson   1948
10. Jack Rowley   1948

10 PLAYERS WHO WON THEIR FIRST ENGLAND CAP WHILST AT OLD TRAFFORD

1.	Johnny Berry	v Argentina	17.05.53
2.	Tommy Taylor	v Argentina	17.05.53
3.	Roger Byrne	v Scotland	03.04.54
4.	Duncan Edwards	v Scotland	02.04.55
5.	Bobby Charlton	v Scotland	19.04.58
6.	Gordon Hill	v Italy	28.05.76
7.	Steve Coppell	v Italy	16.11.76
8.	Andy Cole	v Uruguay	29.03.95
9.	Gary Neville	v Japan	03.06.95
10.	Nicky Butt	v Mexico	29.03.97

Paul Scholes

10 MANCHESTER UNITED PLAYERS CAPPED BY ENGLAND DURING THE 1950s

1. Allenby Chilton
2. Johnny Berry
3. Tommy Taylor
4. Roger Byrne
5. Bill Foulkes
6. Ray Wood
7. Duncan Edwards
8. David Pegg
9. Bobby Charlton
10. Wilf McGuinness

Teddy Sheringham

10 MANCHESTER UNITED PLAYERS CAPPED BY ENGLAND DURING THE 1990s

1. Neil Webb
2. Gary Pallister
3. Paul Parker
4. Lee Sharpe
5. Andy Cole
6. Gary Neville
7. David Beckham
8. Paul Scholes
9. Philip Neville
10. Teddy Sheringham

THE FIRST 10 MANCHESTER UNITED PLAYERS CAPPED AT INTERNATIONAL LEVEL BY SCOTLAND

1.	Alexander Bell	1912
2.	Thomas Miller	1921
3.	Neil McBain	1922
4.	Jimmy Delaney	1947
5.	Denis Law	1962
6.	Pat Crerand	1963
7.	Francis Burns	1969
8.	Martin Buchan	1972
9.	Willie Morgan	1972
10.	Alex Forsyth	1973
	George Graham	1973
	Lou Macari	1973

10 MANCHESTER UNITED PLAYERS CAPPED BY SCOTLAND DURING THE 1970s

1. Denis Law
2. Willie Morgan
3. Martin Buchan
4. Alex Forsyth
5. George Graham
6. Lou Macari
7. Jim Holton
8. Stewart Houston
9. Joe Jordan
10. Gordon McQueen

THE FIRST 10 NEWTON HEATH/MANCHESTER UNITED PLAYERS CAPPED BY WALES AT INTERNATIONAL LEVEL

1. John Doughty   1887
2. John Powell   1887
3. Thomas Burke   1887
4. Joseph Davies   1888
5. Roger Doughty   1888
6. W. Owen   1888
7. George Owen   1889
8. John Owen   1892
9. Caesar Jenkyns   1897
10. William Meredith 1907

10 MORE MANCHESTER UNITED PLAYERS CAPPED AT INTERNATIONAL LEVEL BY WALES

1. Samuel Bennion   1925
2. Thomas Jones   1926
3. Henry Thomas   1927
4. David Williams   1928
5. John Warner   1939
6. Colin Webster   1957
7. Graham Moore   1963
8. Ronald Davies   1972
9. Mickey Thomas   1978
10. Alan Davies   1983

THE FIRST 10 MANCHESTER UNITED PLAYERS CAPPED AT INTERNATIONAL LEVEL BY NORTHERN IRELAND

1. Michael Hamill   1912
2. W. Crooks   1922
3. David Lyner   1922
4. Walter McMillen   1933
5. Thomas Breen   1937
6. Johnny Carey   1946
7. Jackie Blanchflower   1954
8. Harry Gregg   1958
9. James Nicholson   1960
10. William Briggs   1962

10 MORE MANCHESTER UNITED PLAYERS CAPPED AT INTERNATIONAL LEVEL BY NORTHERN IRELAND

1. Trevor Anderson
2. George Best
3. Mal Donaghy
4. Tommy Jackson
5. David McCreery
6. Chris McGrath
7. Sammy McIlroy
8. Jimmy Nicholl
9. Thomas Sloan
10. Norman Whiteside

THE FIRST 10 MANCHESTER UNITED PLAYERS CAPPED AT INTERNATIONAL LEVEL BY THE REPUBLIC OF IRELAND

1. Johnny Carey   1937
2. Thomas Breen   1937
3. Liam Whelan   1956
4. Joseph Carolan   1959
5. Johnny Giles   1959
6. Noel Cantwell   1961
7. Shay Brennan   1965
8. Tony Dunne   1965
9. Pat Dunne   1965
10. Don Givens   1969

10 IRISH MANCHESTER UNITED PLAYERS CAPPED AT INTERNATIONAL LEVEL DURING THE 1960s

1.	George Best	Northern Ireland
2.	Noel Cantwell	Republic of Ireland
3.	William Briggs	Northern Ireland
4.	Shay Brennan	Republic of Ireland
5.	Harry Gregg	Northern Ireland
6.	Don Givens	Republic of Ireland
7.	Samuel McMillan	Northern Ireland
8.	Johnny Giles	Republic of Ireland
9.	James Nicholson	Northern Ireland
10.	Tony Dunne	Republic of Ireland

10 IRISH MANCHESTER UNITED PLAYERS CAPPED AT INTERNATIONAL LEVEL DURING THE 1970s

1.	George Best	Northern Ireland
2.	Shay Brennan	Republic of Ireland
3.	Tony Dunne	Republic of Ireland
4.	Sammy McIlroy	Northern Ireland
5.	Gerry Daly	Republic of Ireland
6.	Mick Martin	Republic of Ireland
7.	Trevor Anderson	Northern Ireland
8.	Paddy Roche	Republic of Ireland
9.	Jimmy Nicholl	Northern Ireland
10.	Ashley Grimes	Republic of Ireland

10 MANCHESTER UNITED PLAYERS WHO HAVE SCORED FOR ENGLAND

1. Stan Pearson
2. Jack Rowley
3. Duncan Edwards
4. Tommy Taylor
5. Bobby Charlton
6. Steve Coppell
7. Stuart Pearson
8. Bryan Robson
9. Ray Wilkins
10. Paul Scholes

10 MANCHESTER UNITED PLAYERS AND THE COUNTRY THEY MADE THEIR INTERNATIONAL DEBUT AGAINST

1.	Nicky Butt (England)	v Mexico
2.	Eric Cantona (France)	v West Germany
3.	Andy Cole (England)	v Uruguay
4.	Denis Irwin (Rep of Ire)	v Morocco
5.	Ryan Giggs (Wales)	v Belgium
6.	Roy Keane (Rep of Ire)	v Chile
7.	Gary Neville (England)	v Japan
8.	Ole Gunnar Solskjaer (Norway)	v Jamaica
9.	Brian McClair (Scotland)	v Luxembourg
10.	Phil Neville (England)	v China

10 MANCHESTER UNITED PLAYERS WHO WON ENGLAND B HONOURS

1.	Gary Bailey	1980
2.	Johnny Berry	1952
3.	Roger Byrne	1953
4.	Duncan Edwards	1954
5.	Brian Greenhoff	1978
6.	Gordon Hill	1978
7.	Bryan Robson	1990
8.	Lee Sharpe	1992
9.	Tommy Taylor	1956
10.	Ray Wood	1954

10 MANCHESTER UNITED PLAYERS WHO WON ENGLAND UNDER-23 HONOURS

1.	John Aston Jnr.	1969
2.	Bobby Charlton	1958
3.	Steve Coppell	1976
4.	Duncan Edwards	1954
5.	Bill Foulkes	1955
6.	Brian Kidd	1967
7.	Albert Scanlon	1958
8.	Maurice Setters	1960
9.	Nobby Stiles	1965
10.	Ray Wood	1954

FIRST 10 MANCHESTER UNITED PLAYERS TO BE CAPPED BY ENGLAND AT UNDER-23 LEVEL

1.	Duncan Edwards	1954
2.	Jeff Whitefoot	1954
3.	Ray Wood	1954
4.	Bill Foulkes	1955
5.	David Pegg	1956
6.	Bobby Charlton	1958
7.	Wilf McGuinness	1958
8.	Albert Scanlon	1958
9.	Maurice Setters	1960
10.	John Chisnall	1963

10 MORE MANCHESTER UNITED ENGLAND UNDER-23 INTERNATIONALS

1.	Nobby Stiles	1965
2.	Brian Kidd	1967
3.	David Sadler	1967
4.	John Aston Jnr.	1969
5.	Paul Edwards	1970
6.	Alan Gowling	1971
7.	Brian Greenhoff	1974
8.	Steve Coppell	1976
9.	Gordon Hill	1976
10.	Stuart Pearson	1976

4 MANCHESTER UNITED PLAYERS WHO WON SCOTLAND UNDER-23 HONOURS

1.	Francis Burns	1968	v England
2.	Jim Holton	1973	v Wales
3.	Alex Forsyth	1974	v Wales
4.	Stewart Houston	1975	v Sweden

3 MANCHESTER UNITED PLAYERS WHO WON WELSH UNDER-23 HONOURS

1.	Ken Morgans	1958	v Scotland
2.	Graham Moore	1963	v England
3.	Clive Griffiths	1974	v England

3 MANCHESTER UNITED PLAYERS WHO WON NORTHERN IRELAND UNDER-23 HONOURS

1.	William Briggs	1962	v Wales
2.	James Nicholson	1962	v Wales
3.	Norman Whiteside	1989	v Republic of Ireland

2 MANCHESTER UNITED PLAYERS WHO WON REPUBLIC OF IRELAND UNDER-23 HONOURS

1.	Patrick Anthony Dunne	1966	v France
2.	Derek Brazil	1989	v Northern Ireland

10 MANCHESTER UNITED PLAYERS WHO WON UNDER-23 CAPS FOR THEIR COUNTRY BEFORE MOVING TO OLD TRAFFORD

1.	Jimmy Greenhoff	England
2.	Albert Quixall	England
3.	Alex Stepney	England
4.	Martin Buchan	Scotland
5.	Pat Crerand	Scotland
6.	Denis Law	Scotland
7.	Lou Macari	Scotland
8.	Willie Morgan	Scotland
9.	Ronald Davies	Wales
10.	Wyn Davies	Wales

3 MANCHESTER UNITED PLAYERS WHO WON UNDER-21 HONOURS WITH SCOTLAND

1.	Arthur Albiston	1976	v Czechoslavakia
2.	Scott McGarvey	1982	v England
3.	Graeme Hogg	1984	v Yugoslavia

3 MANCHESTER UNITED PLAYERS WHO WON UNDER-21 HONOURS WITH NORTHERN IRELAND

1. David McCreery   1978   v Republic of Ireland
2. Jimmy Nicholl   1978   v Republic of Ireland
3. Thomas Sloan   1978   v Republic of Ireland

6 MANCHESTER UNITED PLAYERS WHO WON UNDER-21 HONOURS WITH WALES

1. Jonathan Clark   1978   v Scotland
2. Alan Davies   1981   v France
3. Mark Hughes   1982   v Norway
4. Clayton Blackmore   1983   v Norway
5. Deiniol Graham   1990   v England
6. Ryan Giggs   1991   v Poland

4 MANCHESTER UNITED PLAYERS WHO WON UNDER-21 HONOURS WITH THE REPUBLIC OF IRELAND

1. Ashley Grimes   1978   v Northern Ireland
2. Anthony Whelan   1981   v England
3. Derek Brazil   1986   v Scotland
4. Brian Carey   1992   v Switzerland

10 UNITED PLAYERS WHO HAVE PLAYED IN ENGLAND TRIAL MATCHES

1.   Richard Holden   North v South (1908)
2.   George Wall   Stripes v Whites (1911)
3.   Richard Duckworth   Stripes v Whites (1912)
4.   Charles Roberts   Stripes v Whites (1912)
5.   Robert Beale   North v England (1914)
6.   Arthur Whalley   North v England (1914)
7.   John Mew   North v England (1921)
8.   Joseph Spence   England v The Rest (1927)
9.   John Silcock   The Rest v England (1928)
10. John Griffiths   Possibles v Probables (1936)

In the Stripes v Whites matches, the Whites were the Senior team.

10 PLAYERS WHO WERE CAPPED BY ENGLAND BEFORE THEY JOINED MANCHESTER UNITED

1. Frank Barson
2. Ernest Hine
3. Louis Page
4. Albert Quixall
5. William Rawlings
6. Bryan Robson
7. Teddy Sheringham
8. Ian Storey-Moore
9. Neil Webb
10. Ray Wilkins

10 PLAYERS WHO HAD BEEN CAPPED BY THEIR COUNTRY BEFORE THEY JOINED MANCHESTER UNITED

1. Henning Berg — Norway
2. Eric Cantona — France
3. Harry Gregg — Northern Ireland
4. Nikola Jovanovic — Yugoslavia
5. Andrei Kanchelskis — Russia
6. Denis Law — Scotland
7. Billy Meredith — Wales
8. Jesper Olsen — Denmark
9. Jaap Stam — Holland
10. Frank Stapleton — Republic of Ireland

10 MORE PLAYERS WHO WERE CAPPED BY THEIR COUNTRY BEFORE THEY JOINED MANCHESTER UNITED

1. Noel Cantwell — Republic of Ireland
2. Pat Crerand — Scotland
3. Jordi Cruyff — Holland
4. Ronny Johnsen — Norway
5. Roy Keane — Republic of Ireland
6. Lou Macari — Scotland
7. Karel Poborsky — Czech Republic
8. Peter Schmeichel — Denmark
9. Ole Gunnar Solskjaer — Norway
10. Mickey Thomas — Wales

10 PLAYERS WHO WERE FIRST CAPPED BY THEIR COUNTRY AFTER THEY PLAYED FOR MANCHESTER UNITED

1. Arthur Albiston — Scotland
2. Shay Brennan — Republic of Ireland
3. Nicky Butt — England
4. Gerry Daly — Republic of Ireland
5. Alan Davies — Wales
6. Mark Hughes — Wales
7. Paul McGrath — Republic of Ireland
8. Sammy McIlroy — Northern Ireland
9. Gary Neville — England
10. Norman Whiteside — Northern Ireland

FIRST 11 MANCHESTER UNITED PLAYERS TO HAVE PLAYED IN THE WORLD CUP FINALS

1.	John Aston Snr.	England	1950
2.	Roger Byrne	England	1954
3.	Tommy Taylor	England	1954
4.	Harry Gregg	Northern Ireland	1958
5.	Colin Webster	Wales	1958
6.	Bobby Charlton	England	1962, 1966 and 1970
7.	John Connelly	England	1966
8.	Nobby Stiles	England	1966
9.	Martin Buchan	Scotland	1974
10.	Jim Holton	Scotland	1974
11	Willie Morgan	Scotland	1974

5 MANCHESTER UNITED PLAYERS WHO WERE IN ENGLAND'S 1970 MEXICO WORLD CUP SQUAD

1. Bobby Charlton
2. Brian Kidd
3. David Sadler
4. Alex Stepney
5. Nobby Stiles

10 MANCHESTER UNITED PLAYERS WHO HAVE PLAYED IN A WORLD CUP FINALS FOR ENGLAND

1.	John Aston Snr.	1950
2.	Roger Byrne	1954
3.	Tommy Taylor	1954
4.	Bobby Charlton	1962, 1966 and 1970
5.	John Connelly	1966
6.	Nobby Stiles	1966
7.	Steve Coppell	1982
8.	Bryan Robson	1982, 1986 and 1990
9.	Ray Wilkins	1982
10.	Neil Webb	1990

10 MANCHESTER UNITED PLAYERS WHO WON LESS THAN 5 FULL ENGLAND CAPS DURING THEIR CAREER

1.	Johnny Berry	4 caps
2.	David Sadler	4
3.	Warren Bradley	3
4.	Garry Birtles	3
5.	Allenby Chilton	2
6.	Wilf McGuinness	2
7.	Dennis Viollet	2
8.	Brian Kidd	2
9.	Gary Bailey	2
10.	Peter Davenport	1

10 MANCHESTER UNITED PLAYERS WHO WERE ONLY CAPPED ONCE BY THEIR COUNTRY

1.	Francis Burns	Scotland
2.	Bill Foulkes	England
3.	Stewart Houston	Scotland
4.	Caesar Jenkyns	Wales
5.	David Pegg	England
6.	Mike Phelan	England
7.	Jimmy Rimmer	England
8.	Alex Stepney	England
9.	Ian Storey-Moore	England
10.	Danny Wallace	England

2 MANCHESTER UNITED PLAYERS WHO WERE SENT OFF WHILST PLAYING FOR ENGLAND IN THE WORLD CUP FINALS

1.	Ray Wilkins	v Morocco	Mexico 1986
2.	David Beckham	v Argentina	France 1998

1 MANCHESTER UNITED PLAYER WHO LATER MANAGED ENGLAND

1.	Walter Winterbottom	from 1946-62

3 MANCHESTER UNITED MANAGERS WHO HAVE ALSO MANAGED SCOTLAND

1. Matt Busby
2. Tommy Docherty
3. Alex Ferguson

2 MANCHESTER UNITED PLAYERS WHO LATER MANAGED THE REPUBLIC OF IRELAND

1. Noel Cantwell
2. Johnny Giles

1 MANCHESTER UNITED PLAYER WHO PLAYED IN GREAT BRITAIN'S 1968 OLYMPIC TEAM

1. Alan Gowling

5 POST-WAR CAPTAINS OF ENGLAND WHO HAVE PLAYED FOR MANCHESTER UNITED DURING THEIR CAREER

1. Peter Beardsley
2. Bobby Charlton
3. Paul Ince
4. Bryan Robson
5. Ray Wilkins

3 COUNTRIES ANDREI KANCHELSKIS WON AN INTERNATIONAL CAP WITH DURING HIS OLD TRAFFORD CAREER

1. CIS/USSR
2. Russia
3. Ukraine

15 COUNTRIES WHICH MANCHESTER UNITED PLAYERS HAVE REPRESENTED AT INTERNATIONAL LEVEL

1.	Australia	Mark Bosnich
2.	Czech Republic	Karel Poborsky
3.	Denmark	Peter Schmeichel
4.	England	Bobby Charlton
5.	France	Eric Cantona
6.	Holland	Jaap Stam
7.	Northern Ireland	George Best
8.	Norway	Ole Gunnar Solskjaer
9.	Republic of Ireland	Frank Stapleton
10.	Russia	Andrei Kanchelskis
11.	Scotland	Denis Law
12.	Ukraine	Andrei Kanchelskis
13.	USA	Eddie McIlvenny
14.	Wales	Ryan Giggs
15.	Yugoslavia	Nikola Jovanovic

6 MANCHESTER UNITED PLAYERS WHO WON AMATEUR INTERNATIONAL CAPS FOR ENGLAND

1. Lee Bradbury
2. Warren Bradley
3. Harold Hardman
4. Mike Pinner
5. David Sadler
6. John Walton

A MANCHESTER UNITED TEAM WHICH CONTAINED FULL INTERNATIONALS FROM EIGHT DIFFERENT COUNTRIES

(Manchester United versus Newcastle United, FA Premier League, 29.10.94)

Peter Schmeichel	Denmark
Roy Keane	Republic of Ireland
Denis Irwin	Republic of Ireland
Steve Bruce	Uncapped
Andrei Kanchelskis	Russia
Gary Pallister	England
Eric Cantona	France
Paul Ince	England
Brian McClair	Scotland
Mark Hughes	Wales
Ryan Giggs	Wales
Keith Gillespie (for Giggs)	Northern Ireland

United won 2-0

2 SETS OF NEWTON HEATH/MANCHESTER UNITED BROTHERS WHO WON CAPS FOR THEIR COUNTRY IN THE SAME GAME

1. Jack and Roger Doughty   for Wales   1888
2. Gary and Phil Neville   for England   1996

Philip and Gary Neville

Ronny Johnsen (Norway) is chased by Gorden Durie (Scotland)

5 MANCHESTER UNITED PLAYERS WHO PARTICIPATED IN A COMMONWEALTH INTERNATIONAL

1.	Richard Duckworth	1910 v South Africa
2.	George Wall	1910 v South Africa
3.	Clarence Hilditch	1920 v South Africa
4.	John Mew	1920 v South Africa
5.	Wilfred Woodcock	1920 v South Africa

1 MANCHESTER UNITED PLAYER WHO PARTICIPATED IN A WARTIME INTERNATIONAL

1.	Jack Rowley	1944	for England v Wales

4 MANCHESTER UNITED PLAYERS WHO PLAYED FOR ENGLAND IN AN AMATEUR INTERNATIONAL

1.	Harold Hardman	1908 v Belgium
2.	John Walton	1952 v Northern Ireland
3.	Warren Bradley	1958 v Finland
4.	Michael Pinner	1961 v Rep of Ireland

1 MANCHESTER UNITED PLAYER WHO REPRESENTED THE UNITED KINGDOM IN THE 1908 OLYMPIC GAMES

1.	Harold Hardman

4 MANCHESTER UNITED PLAYERS WHO PLAYED FOR ENGLAND IN AN UNOFFICIAL INTERNATIONAL

1.	Brian Kidd	1970 v Colombia
2.	Nobby Stiles	1970 v Colombia
3.	Brian Greenhoff	1976 v Team America
4.	Stuart Pearson	1976 v Team America

1 MANCHESTER UNITED PLAYER WHO HAS PLAYED FOR A REST OF THE WORLD TEAM

1.	Denis Law	1963 v England

3 MANCHESTER UNITED PLAYERS WHO HAVE PLAYED FOR A REST OF EUROPE TEAM

1.	Johnny Carey	1947 v Great Britain
2.	Bobby Charlton	1964 v Scandanavia
3.	Denis Law	1964 v Scandanavia

10 EVENTS IN OCTOBER

1. 1 OCTOBER 1936
A gentle giant is born
Duncan Edwards (half-back 1952-8) is born in Dudley, Worcestershire.

2. 1 OCTOBER 1995
Eric Cantona returns
Manchester United 2   Liverpool 2
Following his eight-month ban from football, Eric Cantona made his comeback in a Premier League game versus Liverpool at Old Trafford. Nicky Butt fired the Reds ahead in the second minute thanks to a marvellous through ball from the French genius. Robbie Fowler looked set to spoil Eric's return by putting the Merseysiders 2-1 ahead with goals either side of half-time. But the stage was set for Eric and after Ryan Giggs was pulled down in the penalty area, Eric stepped up and cooly placed his spot-kick past an outstretched David James. Eric could not hide his delight and ran to the fans behind the goal to celebrate, where he was engulfed in embraces from his team-mates.

3. 2 OCTOBER 1957
Old Trafford tastes European football for the first time
Manchester United 3   Shamrock Rovers 2
Shamrock Rovers became United's first ever Old Trafford European opponents and victims, in a competitive tie, when the Reds beat them 3-2 in the European Cup.

4. 3 OCTOBER 1891
The beginning of a fierce rivalry
Newton Heath 5   Ardwick 1
This FA Cup first qualifying round game was the first ever Manchester Derby. The Heathens (later to become Manchester United) beat Ardwick (who subsequently became Manchester City) 5-1(scorers: Farman 2, Doughty, Sneddon and Edge).

5. 3 OCTOBER 1981
Atkinson gets his man
Manchester United 5   Wolverhampton Wanderers 0
Having managed Bryan Robson, when he was in charge of West Bromwich Albion, Ron Atkinson finally secured the signature of the twenty-four year old midfielder. Ron Atkinson spoke to Bill Shankly about Robson and the legendary Liverpool manager advised Atkinson to pay whatever it took to get him if he wanted him that much. Atkinson took the advice of Shankly and splashed out a British club record fee of £1,500,000 for his man. Robson signed for the Reds on the Old Trafford pitch prior to the Reds' Division One home game with Wolverhampton Wanderers. United won the game 5-0 (scorers: McIlroy 3, Birtles and Stapleton). After thirteen glorious seasons at the club few would argue that it was money well spent.

6. 5 OCTOBER 1985
100 per cent winning start to season ends
Luton Town 1   Manchester United 1
Luton Town became the first team to take points off the high flying Reds in the 1985-6 season when they held them to a 1-1 (scorer: Hughes) draw at Kenilworth Road. It was the first time in their opening eleven games that the Reds failed to win.

7. 6 OCTOBER 1956
Bobby Charlton makes his United debut
Manchester United 4   Charlton Athletic 2

Bobby Charlton made his United debut against Charlton Athletic, and scored two goals in United's 4-2 (other scorers: Berry and Whelan) victory. In the return game four months later he bagged a hat-trick! Bobby Charlton was a Busby Babe who survived the Munich air disaster and who ten years later helped Matt Busby fulfill his dream of conquering Europe by scoring two of United's four goals in the 1968 European Cup Final. The young Charlton, a nephew of the famous Newcastle United forward, Jackie Milburn, arrived at Old Trafford as an amateur in January 1953. In October 1954 he turned professional for the club and over the next three decades he became one of the greatest players in the club's history. Charlton won FA Youth Cup winners' medals in 1954, 1955 and 1956 and although he wore the No. 9 shirt for United he was more at home in midfield where his surging runs were usually followed by a bullet like shot into the back of the opponents' net. Bobby enjoyed unprecedented success for both club and country. With United he won 3 League Championship medals (1957, 1965 and 1967), an FA Cup winners' medal in 1963 (as well as Finalists' medals in 1957 and 1958) and a European Cup winners' medal in 1968. In 1966 Bobby helped England to World Cup glory and in the same year he was voted European Footballer of the Year. He won 106 caps for his country and holds the record for most England goals, at 49. Along with Best and Law, Charlton brought back the glory years to Old Trafford during the swinging sixties. His 752 appearances and 247 goals for the Reds are both club records which are unlikely to be surpassed in the modern game, where a player's loyalty to his club is not the same as it was in Charlton's era.

Appearances: FL: 604 (2) goals 199 FAC: 79, goals 19 FLC: 24, goals 7 EUR: 45, 22 goals TOTAL: 752 [2], 247 goals.

8. 8 OCTOBER 1926
United boss suspended for irregularities

Manchester United's manager, John Chapman, was suspended by the Football League for alleged management irregularities. Chapman was replaced by Walter Crickmer as secretary whilst Clarence Hilditch assumed the role of caretaker player-manager.

9. 15 OCTOBER 1892
Record football League win
Newton Heath 10   Wolverhampton Wanderers 1

Newton Heath registered their first ever win in League Football with a 10-1 (scorers: Donaldson 3, Stewart 3, Carson, Farman, Hendry and Hood) demolition of Wolverhampton Wanderers in a Division 2 game. It was the Heathens' seventh game of the season, whilst the scoreline was not only the first 10-1 score in League Football but it is also a club record score for a league game.

10. 24 OCTOBER 1927
Saviour of United dies

Newton Heath were in financial difficulties in 1902 and in an effort to raise some much needed capital a Grand Bazaar was held. Harry Stafford, the club's captain, is said to have fastened a barrel around the neck of his St. Bernard dog inviting the crowd to deposit coins in it. The dog is then said to have strayed from the Bazaar and was found by a Mr Thomas. Mr Thomas was the licensee of a hostel owned by Mr Davies, to whom he showed the animal. Mr Davies then purchased the dog as a birthday present for his daughter and installed Stafford as the landlord of one of his public houses. The meeting of Davies and Stafford unquestionably changed the course of the club's history. It was at the meeting of creditors on 18 March 1902 that Harry Stafford advised those in attendance that he knew of four men who were each prepared to invest £500 in the club to rescue it from bankruptcy. John H Davies was one of the four. When Newton Heath subsequently became Manchester United in April 1902, John H Davies was elected the new President. Over the next twenty-five years, until his death, he was the club's saviour in times of financial crisis and along with manager, Ernest Mangnall, John H. Davies brought success to Manchester United. He was also instrumental in the club moving to Old Trafford in 1910.

MONEY GAMES

10 PLAYERS WHO COST UNITED £1MILLION OR MORE

1. Garry Birtles | £1,250,000 | from Nottingham Forest
2. Bryan Robson | £1,500,000 | from West Bromwich Albion
3. Mark Hughes | £1,600,000 | from Barcelona
4. Gary Pallister | £2,300,000 | from Middlesbrough
5. Dion Dublin | £1,000,000 | from Cambridge United
6. Roy Keane | £3,750,000 | from Nottingham Forest
7. Andy Cole | £7,000,000 | from Newcastle United
8. Karel Poborsky | £3,500,000 | from Slavia Prague
9. Teddy Sheringham | £3,500,000 | from Tottenham Hotspur
10. Jaap Stam | £10,750,000 | from PSV Eindhoven

10 PLAYERS PURCHASED BY UNITED FROM LOWER DIVISION SIDES

1. Tommy Taylor | Barnsley
2. Harry Gregg | Doncaster Rovers
3. Ted MacDougall | AFC Bournemouth
4. Steve Coppell | Tranmere Rovers
5. Mickey Thomas | Wrexham
6. Chris Turner | Sunderland
7. Mal Donaghy | Luton Town
8. Lee Sharpe | Torquay United
9. Dion Dublin | Cambridge United
10. Tony Coton | Manchester City

THE FIRST 10 SIX-FIGURE SUMS PAID BY MANCHESTER UNITED FOR A PLAYER

1. Denis Law | £115,000 from Torino | July 1962
2. Willie Morgan | £110,000 from Burnley | August 1968
3. Martin Buchan | £120,000 from Aberdeen | February 1972
4. Ian Storey-Moore | £200,000 from Nott. Forest | March 1972
5. Ted MacDougall | £200,000 from Bournemouth | September 1972
6. George Graham | £120,000 from Arsenal | December 1972
7. Alex Forsyth | £120,000 from Partick Thistle | December 1972
8. Lou Macari | £200,000 from Glasgow Celtic | January 1973
9. Stuart Pearson | £200,000 from Hull City | May 1974
10. Jimmy Greenhoff | £120,000 from Stoke City | November 1976

10 PLAYERS PURCHASED BY UNITED DURING THE 1970S WHO COST THE REDS £100,000 OR MORE

1. Ian Storey-Moore   from Nottingham Forest   £200,000
2. George Graham   from Arsenal   £120,000
3. Alex Forsyth   from Partick Thistle   £100,000
4. Lou Macari   from Glasgow Celtic   £190,000
5. Stuart Pearson   from Hull City   £200,000
6. Jimmy Greenhoff   from Stoke City   £100,000
7. Joe Jordan   from Leeds United   £350,000
8. Gordon McQueen   from Leeds United   £450,000
9. Mickey Thomas   from Wrexham   £300,000
10. Ray Wilkins   from Chelsea   £700,000

10 PLAYERS PURCHASED BY UNITED DURING THE 1970S WHO COST THE REDS LESS THAN £100,000

1. Jim Holton   from Shrewsbury Town   £91,000
2. Mick Martin   from Bohemians   £25,000
3. Gerry Daly   from Bohemians   £22,000
4. Paddy Roche   from Shelbourne   £15,000
5. Stewart Houston   from Brentford   £45,000
6. Jim McCalliog   from Wolverhampton Wanderers   £60,000
7. Ron Davies   from Portsmouth   £43,000
8. Steve Coppell   from Tranmere Rovers   £60,000
9. Gordon Hill   from Millwall   £85,000
10. Chris McGrath   from Tottenham Hotspur   £30,000

7 PLAYERS MANCHESTER UNITED PAID A BRITISH REORD TRANSFER FEE FOR

1. Albert Quixall   from Sheffield Wednesday   £45,000   September 53
2. Denis Law   from Torino   £115,000   July 62
3. Gordon McQueen   from Leeds United   £450,000   February 78
4. Bryan Robson   from West Brom. Albion   £1,500,000   October 81
5. Gary Pallister   from Middlesbrough   £2,300,000   August 89
6. Roy Keane   from Nottingham Forest   £3,750,000   July 93
7. Andy Cole   from Newcastle United   £7,000,000   January 95

NAME GAMES

10 JOHNS WHO HAVE PLAYED FOR MANCHESTER UNITED

1.	John Aston Jnr.	Forward	1964-72
2.	John Aston Snr.	Full-Back	1946-54
3.	John Gidman	Full-Back	1981-86
4.	John Hanlon	Forward	1938-49
5.	John Mew	Goalkeeper	1912-26
6.	John Roach	Full-Back	1945-46
7.	John Silcock	Full-Back	1919-34
8.	John Sivebaek	Full-Back	1985-87
9.	John Walton	Forward	1951-52
10.	John Whittle	Forward	1931-32

10 DAVIDS WHO HAVE PLAYED FOR MANCHESTER UNITED

1.	David Bain	Forward	1922-24
2.	David Beckham	Midfielder	1992-
3.	David Christie	Forward	1908-09
4.	David Ellis	Forward	1923-24
5.	David Herd	Forward	1961-68
6.	David Jones	Half-Back	1937-38
7.	David McCreery	Midfielder	1975-79
8.	David Pegg	Forward	1952-58
9.	David Sadler	Utility	1963-74
10.	David Wallace	Forward	1989-93

10 ARTHURS WHO HAVE PLAYED FOR MANCHESTER UNITED

1.	Arthur Allman	Full-Back	1914-15
2.	Arthur Beadsworth	Forward	1902-03
3.	Arthur Black	Forward	1930-34
4.	Arthur Cashmore	Forward	1913-14
5.	Arthur Chesters	Goalkeeper	1929-32
6.	Arthur Graham	Forward	1983-85
7.	Arthur Hooper	Forward	1909-14
8.	Arthur Lochhead	Forward	1921-26
9.	Arthur Potts	Forward	1913-20
10.	Arthur Whalley	Half-Back	1909-20

10 THOMASES WHO HAVE PLAYED FOR MANCHESTER UNITED

1.	Thomas Arkesden	Forward	1902-06
2.	Thomas Baldwin	Forward	1974-75
3.	Thomas Bamford	Forward	1934-38
4.	Thomas Blackstock	Full-Back	1903-07
5.	Thomas Bogan	Forward	1949-51
6.	Thomas Boyle	Forward	1928-30
7.	Thomas Breen	Goalkeeper	1936-39
8.	Thomas Gipps	Half-Back	1912-15
9.	Thomas Sloan	Midfielder	1978-81
10.	Thomas Taylor	Forward	1953-58

10 FRANCISES OR FRANKS WHO HAVE PLAYED FOR MANCHESTER UNITED

1.	Frank Barson	Half-Back	1922-28
2.	Frank Brett	Full-Back	1921-22
3.	Francis Burns	Defender	1967-72
4.	Frank Clempson	Forward	1949-53
5.	Francis Harris	Half-Back	1920-22
6.	Frank Haydock	Half-Back	1960-63
7.	Frank Hodges	Forward	1919-21
8.	Frank Kopel	Full-Back	1967-69
9.	Frank Stapleton	Forward	1981-87
10.	Frank Williams	Half-Back	1930-31

10 NEWTON HEATH OR MANCHESTER UNITED PLAYERS WITH UNUSUAL NAMES

1.	Alphonso Ainsworth	Inside-Forward	1934-35
2.	Beaumont Asquith	Forward	1939-40
3.	Herbert Birchenough	Goalkeeper	1902-03
4.	Horace Blew	Full-Back	1905-06
5.	Allenby Chilton	Half-Back	1939-55
6.	Levi Draycott	Half-Back	1896-99
7.	Gilbert Godsmark	Forward	1899-1900
8.	Augustine Grimes	Midfielder	1977-83
9.	Proctor Hall	Forward	1903-04
10.	Clarence Hilditch	Half-Back	1919-32

10 MORE NEWTON HEATH OR MANCHESTER UNITED PLAYERS WITH UNUSUAL NAMES

1.	Caesar Jenkyns	Half-Back	1896-98
2.	Hubert Lappin	Forward	1900-03
3.	Norbert Lawton	Half-Back	1959-63
4.	Leslie Lievesley	Half-Back	1931-32
5.	Luigi Macari	Forward	1972-84
6.	Guiliano Maiorana	Forward	1988-89
7.	Joseph Myerscough	Forward	1920-23
8.	Percy Newton	Half-Back	1933-34
9.	Ernest Payne	Forward	1908-09
10.	Lancelot Richardson	Goalkeeper	1925-29

10 MORE WILLIAMS WHO HAVE PLAYED FOR MANCHESTER UNITED

1.	William Dennis	Full-Back	1923-24
2.	William Fielding	Goalkeeper	1946-47
3.	William Foulkes	Defender	1952-70
4.	William Goodwin	Forward	1920-22
5.	William Grassam	Forward	1903-05
6.	William Hartwell	Forward	1903-05
7.	William Henderson	Forward	1921-25
8.	William Hunter	Forward	1912-13
9.	William Whelan	Forward	1954-58
10.	William Morgan	Forward	1968-75

10 WILLIAMS WHO HAVE PLAYED FOR MANCHESTER UNITED

1.	William Bainbridge	Forward	1945-46
2.	William Ball	Half-Back	1902-03
3.	William Behan	Goalkeeper	1933-34
4.	William Berry	Forward	1906-09
5.	William Boyd	Forward	1934-35
6.	William Briggs	Goalkeeper	1960-62
7.	William Bryant	Forward	1934-40
8.	William Bunce	Full-Back	1902-03
9.	William Chalmers	Forward	1932-34
10.	William Chapman	Forward	1926-28

10 MANCHESTER UNITED PLAYERS WHOSE FIRST NAME AND SURNAME BEGIN WITH THE SAME LETTER

1. Arthur Albiston
2. Arthur Allman
3. Brian Birch
4. Dion Dublin
5. George Gladwin
6. George Graham
7. Harold Halse
8. Joe Jordan
9. Paul Parker
10. Walter Winterbottom

10 WILLIAMS WHO HAVE PLAYED FOR NEWTON HEATH

1.	William Booth	Forward	1900-01
2.	William Brooks	Forward	1896-99
3.	William Brown	Forward	1896-97
4.	William Bryant	Forward	1896-1900
5.	William Campbell	Forward	1893-94
6.	William Davidson	Half-Back	1893-95
7.	William Douglas	Goalkeeper	1893-96
8.	William Dunn	Forward	1897-98
9.	William Griffiths	Half-Back	1898-1905
10.	William Gyves	Goalkeeper	1890-91

10 MANCHESTER UNITED MIDDLE NAMES

1. Stewart Mackie Houston
2. Leslie Brown Hofton
3. Maurice Edgar Setters
4. Reginald Lloyd Halton
5. Joseph Bertram Ford
6. Alexander Downie Dawson
7. Herbert Redvers Cartman
8. Martin McLean Buchan
9. William Todd Stewart
10. Frank Drury Mann

10 MORE MANCHESTER UNITED MIDDLE NAMES

1. Joseph Waters Spence
2. Thomas Gable Smith
3. Sammy Baxter McIlroy
4. Peter Boleslaw Schmeichel
5. Carlo Domenico Sartori
6. Henry Bowater Rowley
7. David Middleton Robbin
8. Lancelot Holliday Richardson
9. Reginald Openshaw Lawson
10. Arnoldus Johannus Hyacinthus Muhren

10 MANCHESTER UNITED PLAYERS WITH WILLIAM FOR A SECOND NAME

1. Roger William Byrne
2. James William Kelly
3. Arthur William Lochhead
4. Noel William McFarlane
5. Alexander William Menzies
6. John William Mew
7. Charles William Moore
8. George William Nevin
9. Steven William Paterson
10. Charles William Ramsden

10 MANCHESTER UNITED GOALKEEPERS WHOSE SURNAME BEGINS WITH THE LETTER B

1. Herbert Birchenough — 1902-03
2. Herebert Broomfield — 1908
3. Robert Beale — 1912-15
4. Billy Behan — 1934
5. Jack Breedon — 1935-43
6. Tommy Breen — 1936-43
7. Berry Brown — 1948
8. Ronnie Briggs — 1960-62
9. Gary Bailey — 1978-87
10. Mark Bosnich — 1989-91

3 MANCHESTER UNITED PLAYERS WHOSE SURNAME IS A COUNTRY

1. Joe Jordan
2. Alan Brazil
3. Derek Brazil

7 NEWTON HEATH/MANCHESTER UNITED PLAYERS WITH FAMOUS NAMESAKES

1. Alexander Bell
2. James Bond
3. William Booth
4. James Brown
5. John Morris
6. John Walton
7. Frank Williams

3 MANCHESTER UNITED PLAYERS WHOSE NAME IS A COLOUR

1. Arthur Black
2. Wesley Brown
3. Robert Green

5 NEWTON HEATH/MANCHESTER UNITED PLAYERS WHOSE NAME IS EDIBLE

1. Johnny Berry
2. Joseph Curry
3. Robert Leslie Olive
4. Stephen Pears
5. Francis Pepper

5 SURNAMES THAT RESEMBLE CITIES OR TOWNS

1. Reginald Chester
2. Dion Dublin
3. Stewart Houston
4. Stephen Preston
5. Dwight Yorke

3 SURNAMES THAT RESEMBLE RACECOURSES

1. Reginald Chester
2. Frank Haydock
3. Dwight Yorke

4 SURNAMES THAT YOU CAN ALSO DRIVE

1. John Aston
2. Joseph Ford
3. Willie Morgan
4. John Morris

3 MUSCIAL MANCHESTER UNITED PLAYERS

1. Dion Dublin   Saxophone
2. Lee Sharpe   Drums
3. Peter Schmeichel   Keyboards

5 PLAYERS WHO BECAME HOTELIERS/PUBLICANS

1. Frank Barson
2. Pat Crerand
3. Harry Gregg
4. Billy Meredith
5. Harry Stafford

2 PLAYERS WHO PLAY WITH THEIR COLLARS TURNED UP

1. Eric Cantona
2. Dwight Yorke

Dwight Yorke

18 PLAYERS WHOSE SURNAME COULD ALSO BE A FIRST NAME

1. John Thomas Allan
2. William Dennis
3. Ian Richard Donald
4. William Douglas
5. George Graham
6. Henry Harry Gregg
7. Steven Robert James
8. William Ronald John
9. Edwin Lee
10. Harry Doxford Leonard
11. Edward Lewis
12. Lee Andrew Martin
13. George Owen
14. David Robbie
15. James Ryan
16. Michael Thomas
17. Ernest Vincent
18. Mark Wilson

10 EVENTS IN NOVEMBER

1. 1 NOVEMBER 1930
Reds finally put end to losing streak
Manchester United 2   Birmingham City 0

United lost their opening 12 games of the 1930-31 season in Division One. In this their thirteenth League match, they finally brought the worst run of defeats in the club's history to an end with a 2-0 (scorers: Gallimore and Rowley) home win over Birmingham City. By the end of the season the Reds had lost twenty-seven (nine at home) of their forty-two league games, the worst sequence in the club's history, and it was no surprise that they were relegated to Division Two.

2. 3 NOVEMBER 1894
First Manchester League derby game
Manchester City 2   Newton Heath 5

This was the first ever Football League encounter between the two Manchester giants. City had just changed their name from Ardwick whilst it would be eight more years before Newton Heath became Manchester United. The Heathens had just been relegated and 14,000 fans, despite the poor weather, turned up to watch the game. Billy Meredith, who later played for United, was making his City debut but he couldn't stop the Heathens running out 5-2 victors. Richard Smith scored four times for the Heathens, the first time a player had scored four goals in a single game for the club. The game was played at City's Hyde Road ground.

3. 5 NOVEMBER 1921
John Chapman takes charge of his first game
Manchester United 3   Middlesbrough 5

John Chapman, who replaced John Robson as the manager of Manchester United, took charge of his first game as the new boss. Chapman's reign got off to a bad start when the Reds were beaten 5-3 (scorers: Lochhead, Sapsford and Spence) in a Division One game at Old Trafford. Chapman was a Scot who had been manager of Airdrieonians for fifteen years before moving to Old Trafford. At the end of his first season in charge United finished bottom of the First Division and were relegated to Division Two where they remained until season 1925-6. In October 1926 Chapman was suspended by the Football Association for alleged improper conduct. The United Board felt they had no option but to sack him and to this day the reasons for his suspension remain a mystery.

4. 6 NOVEMBER 1971
McIlroy scores on his debut
Manchester City 3   Manchester United 3

United and City drew 3-3 (scorers: Gowling, Kidd and McIlroy) at Maine Road in the first Manchester Derby of the 1971-72 season. McIlroy, who signed for United as a fifteen-year-old apprentice, made a dream start to his United career by opening the scoring in front of 63,326 fans. McIlroy was a tremendous servant to the Reds playing almost 400 games for the club. He appeared in three FA Cup Finals with United (1976, 1977 and 1979) and was a member of United's 1974-75 Division 2 Championship winning team. In February 1982 he left Old Trafford after nearly eleven years and joined Stoke City for £350,000.

5. 6 NOVEMBER 1986
Fergie's reign begins

Alex Ferguson left Aberdeen to take up his appointment as the new manager of Manchester United. Alex Ferguson was the man responsible for breaking the Glasgow domination of Scottish football with his Aberdeen team which conquered both the domestic and European scene. It took Alex four years to win a trophy at Old Trafford when United won the 1990 FA Cup but since 1990 United have dominated the English game, enjoying unprecedented success. Under Alex Ferguson United have been: Premier League Champions 1993, 1994, 1996, 1997; Premier League Runners-Up 1998; Division 1 Runners-Up 1988, 1992; FA Cup Winners 1990, 1994, 1996; FA Cup Finalists 1995; League Cup Winners 1992; League Cup Finalists 1991, 1994; Double Winners 1994, 1996; European Cup-Winners' Cup Winners 1991; European Super Cup Winners 1991; Charity Shield Winners 1990 (Joint), 1993, 1994, 1996, 1997.

6. 7 NOVEMBER 1981
Coppell sets club appearance record
Sunderland 1   Manchester United 5
Steve Coppell set the club record for appearances when he played his 206th consecutive League game for the Reds in their 5-1 (scorers: Stapleton 2, Birtles, Moran and Robson) win over Sunderland at Roker Park. Coppell's run of appearances began on 15 January 1977 in United's 2-0 (scorer: Macari 2) home win over Coventry City.

7. 10 NOVEMBER 1994
Blue Moon Murder
Manchester United 5   Manchester City 0
United were in scintillating form for the visit of neighbours, City. Eric Cantona opened the scoring for the Reds whilst Andrei Kanchelskis scored the first hat-trick in a Manchester Derby for twenty-four years. (Mark Hughes was the other United goalscorer.) Andrei's hat-trick is the first hat-trick by any United player since Mark Hughes scored three goals against Millwall in September 1989 and the first hat-trick by a Red in a Derby game since Alex Dawson scored a hat-trick in United's 5-1 demolition of City on New Year's Eve 1960.

8. 19 NOVEMBER 1991
European Super Cup Final
Manchester United 1 Red Star Belgrade 0
The meeting between the European Cup winners and the European Cup-Winners' Cup winners is normally played over two legs on a home and away basis. Because of the problems in Yugoslavia at this time it was decided to play only one match for the 1991 trophy. The game was played at Old Trafford, United winning the Cup 1-0 thanks to a Brian McClair goal. The United line-up was as follows: Schmeichel, Irwin, Martin (Giggs), Bruce, Webb, Pallister, Kanchelskis, Ince, McClair, Hughes, Blackmore.

9. 20 NOVEMBER 1971
Law celebrates his 200th appearance for the Reds
Manchester United 3 Leicester City 2
Denis Law marked his 200th appearance for the Reds with two goals in United's 3-2 home win over Leicester City in a First Division game. (The other scorer was Brian Kidd).

10. 22 NOVEMBER 1986
United record their first win under Ferguson
Manchester United 1 Queens Park Rangers 0
Following a defeat and a draw Alex Ferguson finally tasted victory as the new Manchester United manager when the Reds beat Queens Park Rangers 1-0 at Old Trafford in a First Division game. John Sivebaek was the goalscorer.

SEEING RED

10 SCOTSMEN SENT OFF PLAYING FOR UNITED

1. Alexander Sandy Turnbull   v Manchester City (h) on 21 December 1907
2. James McLachlan Turnbull   v Aston Villa (h) on 16 October 1909
3. Thomas Frame   v Port Vale (a) on 29 October 1932
4. David George Herd   v Willem II (ECWC) (a) on 25 September 1963
5. Denis Law   v Blackpool (a) on 14 November 1964
6. Pat Crerand   v Partizan Belgrade (EC) (h) on 19 April 1966
7. John Fitzpatrick   v AC Milan (EC) (a) on 23 April 1969
8. James Holton   v Newcastle United (h) on 17 March 1973
9. Lou Macari   v Manchester City (a) on 13 March 1974
10. Gordon McQueen   v Stockport County (FLC) (h) on 30 August 1978

10 ENGLISHMEN SENT OFF PLAYING FOR UNITED

1. Enoch James West   v Aston Villa (a) on 22 April 1911
2. James Hanson   v Aston Villa (a) on 27 August 1928
3. Charles William Moore   v Leicester City (a) on 2 September 1929
4. Henry Cockburn   v Manchester City (h) on 3 September 1949
5. Allenby Chilton   v Manchester City (FAC) (a) on 29 January 1955
6. Brian Kidd   v Tottenham Hotspur (FAC) (a) on 13 January 1968
7. Brian Greenhoff   v Carlisle United (FAC) (a) on 7 January 1978
8. Remi Moses   v Arsenal (a) on 2 May 1983
9. Steve Bruce   v Derby County (h) on 13 January 1990
10. Nicky Butt   v West Ham United (a) on 22 January 1996

10 IRISHMEN SENT OFF PLAYING FOR UNITED

1. Joseph Carolan   v Bayern Munich (FR) (a) on 8 August 1959
2. Noel Cantwell   v Eintracht Frankfurt (FR) (a) on 13 August 1963
3. Harry Gregg   v Blackburn Rovers (h) on 6 November 1965
4. George Best   v Chelsea (a) on 18 August 1971
5. Tony Dunne   v Wolverhampton Wanderers (FAC) (a) on 13 January 1973
6. Sammy McIlroy   v Bristol City (a) on 7 May 1977
7. Ashley Grimes   v West Ham United (a) on 30 October 1982
8. Kevin Moran   v Everton (FAC Final) on 18 May 1985
9. Liam O'Brien   v Southampton (a) on 3 January 1987
10. Roy Keane   v Middlesbrough (h) on 28 October 1995

10 UNITED PLAYERS SENT OFF AGAINST FOREIGN OPPONENTS

1. Brian Birch   v Aalburg (FR) (a) on 29 May 1951
2. Albert Quixall   v Bayern Munich (FR) (a) on 8 August 1959
3. Maurice Setters   v Mallorca (FR) (a) on 16 May 1962
4. Pat Crerand   v Ferencvaros (ICFC) (a) on 5 June 1965
5. Nobby Stiles   v F.K. Austria (FR) (a) on 12 August 1966
6. Denis Law   v Western Australia (FR) (a) on 27 June 1967
7. George Best   v Estudiantes (WCC) (h) on 16 October 1968
8. Lou Macari   v Real Murcia (FR) (a) on 18 August 1973
9. Eric Cantona   v Galatasaray (ECC) (a) on 3 November 1993
10. Paul Ince   v Gothenburg (ECL) (a) on 23 November 1994

10 MANCHESTER UNITED PLAYERS WHO WERE SENT OFF IN A FRIENDLY

1. Colin Webster   v Young Boys Berne (h)   01.10.58
2. Albert Quixall   v Bayern Munich (a)   08.08.59
3. Joe Carolan   v Bayern Munich (a)   08.08.59
4. Noel Cantwell   v Eintracht Frankfurt (a)   13.08.63
5. Nobby Stiles   v FK Austria (a)   12.08.66
6. Denis Law   v Western Australia (a)   27.06.67
7. Lou Macari   v Real Murcia (a)   18.08.73
8. Gordon McQueen   v Ajax Amsterdam (a)   14.08.83
9. Bryan Robson   v Arsenal (a)   25.07.93
10. Eric Cantona   v Glasgow Rangers (a)   06.08.94

2 MANCHESTER UNITED PLAYERS WHO WERE SENT OFF IN A CUP FINAL

1. Kevin Moran   FA Cup Final   1985
2. Andrei Kanchelskis   League Cup Final   1994

2 CONSECUTIVE GAMES IN WHICH ERIC CANTONA WAS SENT OFF WHILST PLAYING FOR MANCHESTER UNITED

1. v Swindon Town (a)   FA Carling Premier League   19.03.94
2. v Arsenal (a)   FA Carling Premier League   22.03.94

1 MANCHESTER UNITED PLAYER WHO WAS SENT OFF IN HIS DEBUT GAME FOR THE CLUB

1. Pat McGibbon v York City (h)   League Cup, R2 1st leg   20.09.95

3 MANCHESTER UNITED PLAYERS WHO WERE SENT OFF PLAYING AGAINST MANCHESTER CITY

1. Alexander Sandy Turnbull (h)   Division 1   21.12.07
2. Henry Cockburn (h)   Division 1   03.09.49
3. Allenby Chilton (a)   FA Cup   29.01.55
4. Lou Macari (a)   Division 1   13.03.74

10 MANCHESTER UNITED PLAYERS SENT OFF IN THE FA CUP

1. Billy Meredith   v Brighton & Hove Albion (h)   Round 1   16.01.09
2. Allenby Chilton   v Manchester City (a)   Round 4   29.01.55
3. Brian Kidd   v Spurs (a)   Round 3 Replay   13.01.68
4. Tony Dunne   v Wolves (a)   Round 3   13.01.73
5. Brian Greenhoff   v Carlisle United (a)   Round 3   07.01.78
6. Kevin Moran   v Everton (W)   Final   18.05.85
7. Bryan Robson   v Sunderland (a)   Round 4   25.01.86
8. Mark Hughes   v Sheffield United (a)   Round 3   09.01.94
9. Peter Schmeichel   v Charlton Athletic (h)   Round 6   12.03.94
10. Roy Keane   v Crystal Palace (n)   S-Final Replay   12.04.95

Game 6 was played at Wembley

3 MANCHESTER UNITED PLAYERS SENT OFF IN THE LEAGUE CUP

1. Gordon McQueen   v Stockport County (h)   Round 2   30.08.78
2. Andrei Kanchelskis   v Aston Villa (W)   Final   27.03.94
3. Pat McGibbon   v York City (h)   R2, 1st leg   20.09.95

Game 1 was played at Old Trafford

Game 2 was played at Wembley

Game 3 was Pat McGibbon's debut for the club

1 MANCHESTER UNITED PLAYER SENT OFF IN THE EUROPEAN CUP-WINNERS' CUP

1. David Herd   v Willem II (a)   Round 1, 1st leg   25.09.63

1 MANCHESTER UNITED PLAYER SENT OFF IN THE UEFA CUP

1. Mark Hughes   v Torpedo Moscow (a)   Round 1, 2nd leg   29.09.92

3 MANCHESTER UNITED PLAYERS SENT OFF IN THE EUROPEAN CUP

1.	John Fitzpatrick	v AC Milan (a)	Semi-Final, 1st leg 23.04.69
2.	Eric Cantona	v Galatasaray (a)	Round 2, 2nd leg 03.11.93
3.	Paul Ince	v Gothenburg (a)	Group Game 23.11.94

Game 3 : UEFA Champions League

5 WELSH PLAYERS SENT OFF WHILST PLAYING FOR MANCHESTER UNITED

1.	Billy Merdith	v Brighton & Hove Albion (h)	16.01.09
2.	Colin Webster	v Young Boys Berne (h)	01.10.58
3.	Mickey Thomas	v Bochum (a)	01.08.79
4.	Mark Hughes	v Sunderland (a)	24.11.84
5.	Colin Gibson	v Liverpool (a)	04.04.88
6.	Mark Hughes	v Liverpool (h)	06.10.91
7.	Mark Hughes	v Moscow Torpedo (a)	29.09.92
8.	Mark Hughes	v Sheffield United (a)	09.01.94
9.	Mark Hughes	v Arsenal (a)	26.11.94

10 EVENTS IN DECEMBER

1. 1 DECEMBER 1906
United taste defeat in the first ever Division 1 Derby
Manchester City 3 Manchester United 0
United's neighbours, City, defeated them 3-0 in the first ever Division One meeting between the two clubs.

2. 3 DECEMBER 1904
Best ever sequence of League wins without conceding a goal
Manchester United 1 Doncaster Rovers 0
United recorded their best ever sequence of League wins, without conceding a goal, when they beat Doncaster Rovers 1-0 (scorer: Peddie) at Old Trafford in a Division Two game. The win was the Reds' seventh successive victory during the 1904-5 season.

3. 6 DECEMBER 1992
Eric's League debut
Manchester United 2 Manchester City 1
Following his transfer from Leeds United Eric Cantona made his League debut for United as a second half substitute for Ryan Giggs in the Reds 2-1 derby win over Manchester City (scorers: Ince and Hughes). Eric's arrival at Old Trafford was the catalyst for United's huge success during the nineties. With the Reds Eric won four FA Carling Premier League Championships, two FA Cups (including 2 doubles) and four FA Charity Shields.

Appearances: PL: 142 (1), goals 64 FAC: 17, goals 10 FLC: 6, goals 1 EUR: 16, goals 5 TOTAL: 181 (1) apps, 80 goals.

4. 16 DECEMBER 1972
O'Farrell's reign is close to an end
Frank O' Farrell's last game in charge of United ended in defeat when United were hammered 5-0 by Crystal Palace at Selhurst Park. The man who was about to succeed him as manager, Tommy Docherty, was watching from the stands. After the game Sir Matt Busby approached Docherty to enquire whether or not he was interested in managing United. Docherty indicated that he had wanted the job for the last twenty-five years.

5. 16 DECEMBER 1983
BBC screen first ever live Match Of The Day
Manchester United 4 Tottenham Hotspur 2
BBC Television's cameras visited Old Trafford to screen the first ever live Match of the Day. In an exciting game the Reds won 4-2 with goals from Arthur Graham (2) and Kevin Moran (2).

6. 19 DECEMBER 1972
Frank O'Farrell is sacked and George Best resigns
Manchester United's Board of Directors met at the offices of Chairman, Louis Edwards, and made their decision to sack the management team of Frank O'Farrell, Malcolm Musgrove and John Aston. They issued the following statement: 'In view of the poor position in the League, it was unanimously decided that Mr O'Farrell, Malcolm

Musgrove and John Aston be relieved of their duties.' The Board's statement also went on to say. 'Furthermore, George Best will remain on the transfer list and will not be selected again for Manchester United as it is felt it is in the best interest of the club and the player that he leaves Old Trafford.' A few hours later George Best handed in his letter of resignation.

Tommy Docherty takes charge at Old Trafford

A few hours after O'Farrell's sacking Tommy Docherty was unveiled as the new manager of Manchester United. Docherty had already gained managerial experience at Chelsea, Aston Villa, Queens Park Rangers, Rotherham United and Oporto of Portugal. He was a breath of fresh air to the United faithful on the terraces and did a remarkable job of steering the team away from the relegation zone. As it turned out Docherty was only putting off the inevitable because at the end of the following season, 1973-74, United were relegated to Division 2. However, the spell in the lower Division enabled Docherty to blood many new young players and the team adopted a swashbuckling style which culminated in the Division 2 Championship during season 1974-75. United were back and the crowds poured into Old Trafford to watch one of the most exciting teams for many a season. In their first season back in the top flight United finished third in the League and lost the 1976 FA Cup Final to Southampton. Under Docherty United returned to Wembley the following year and this time they came away with the trophy having defeated Liverpool 2-1 and thereby depriving the Merseysiders of the Double.

7.   26 DECEMBER 1899
Newton Heath set the club's record away win
Grimsby Town 0 Newton Heath 7

In a Division Two game Newton Heath set the club's record away victory when they defeated Grimsby Town 7-0 (scorers: Bryant 2, Cassidy 2, Jackson, Parkinson and 1 own goal).

8.   27 DECEMBER 1920
Record home attendance
Manchester United 1 Aston Villa 3

United set their record home attendance for a game at Old Trafford when a crowd of 70,504 poured into the stadium for their Division One game against Aston Villa. Sadly for the home fans the Reds lost the game 1-3 (scorer: Harrison).

9.   28TH DECEMBER 1963
George Best opens his united goalscoring account
Manchester United 5 Burnley 1

George Best scored his first goal for United in the 5-1 home win over Burnley (other scorers: Herd 2 and Moore 2).

10.   31 DECEMBER 1994
Fergie Awarded CBE

Alex Ferguson was awarded a CBE in the New Year's Honours List.

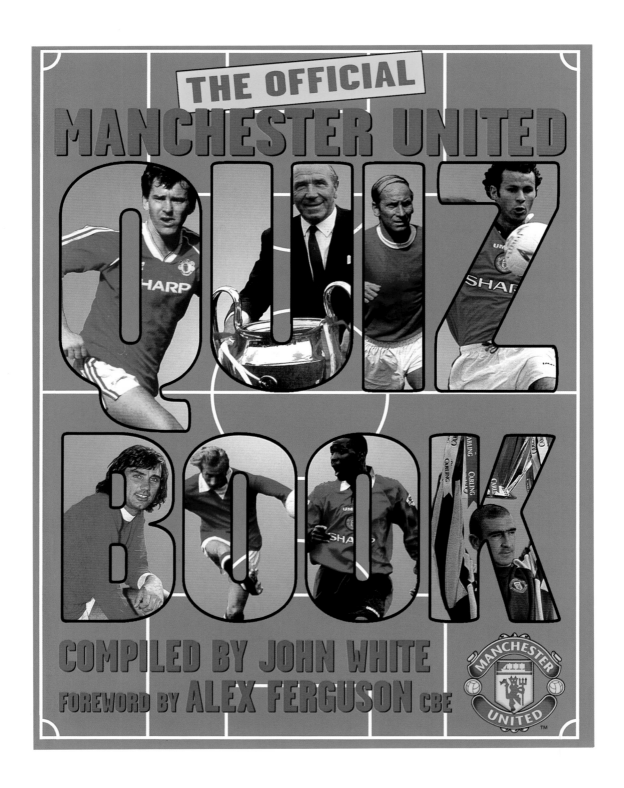

THE OFFICIAL MANCHESTER UNITED QUIZ BOOK
0 233 99417 3 £9.99

THE OFFICIAL
MANCHESTER
UNITED
ILLUSTRATED
ENCYCLOPEDIA

With a Foreword
by Sir Bobby
Charlton

THE OFFICIAL MANCHESTER UNITED ILLUSTRATED ENCYCLOPEDIA
0 233 99155 7   £25.00

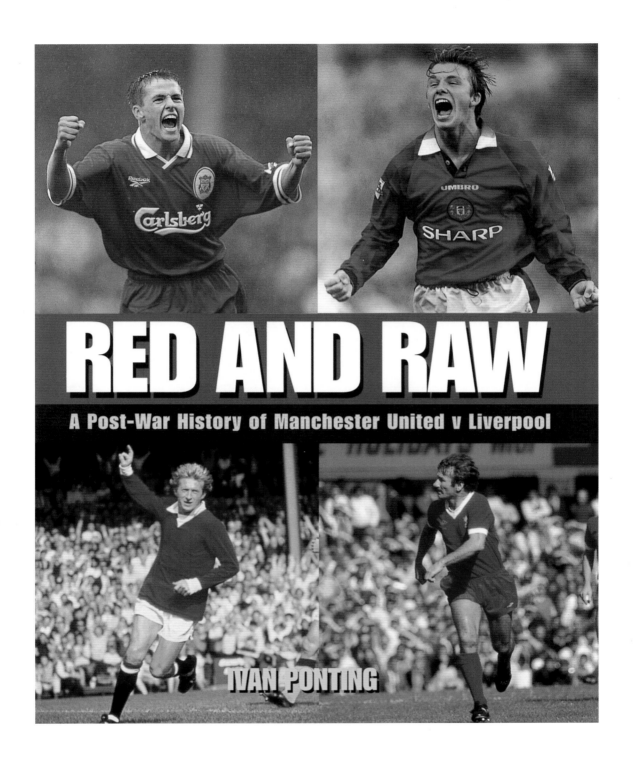

RED AND RAW

A Post-War History of Manchester United v Liverpool

IVAN PONTING

RED AND RAW
0 233 99369 X   £14.99

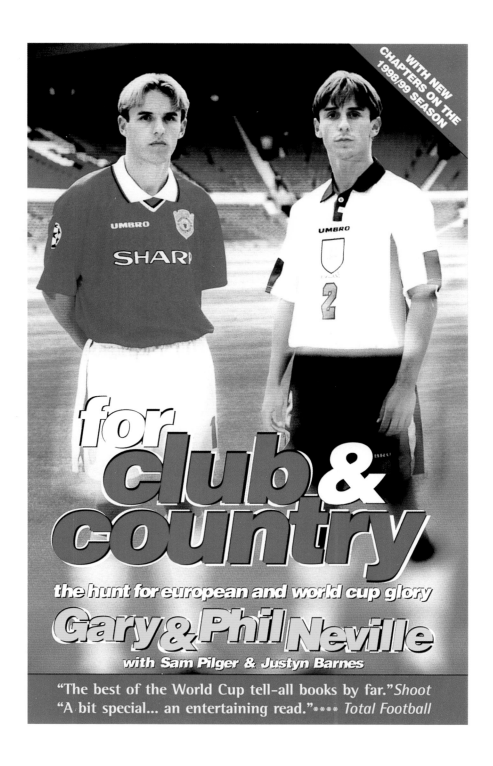

WITH NEW CHAPTERS ON THE 1998/99 SEASON

for club & country

the hunt for european and world cup glory

Gary & Phil Neville

with Sam Pilger & Justyn Barnes

"The best of the World Cup tell-all books by far." *Shoot*
"A bit special... an entertaining read." **** *Total Football*

FOR CLUB AND COUNTRY
0 233 99498 X   £6.99

OTHER TITLES AVAILABLE FROM MANCHESTER UNITED BOOKS

0 233 99045 3	**Cantona on Cantona**	£14.99
0 233 99047 X	**Alex Ferguson: Ten Glorious Years**	£9.99
0 233 99046 1	**Ryan Giggs: Genius at Work**	£9.99
0 233 99362 2	**Odd Man Out: A Player's Diary by Brian McClair**	£6.99
0 233 99178 6	**Manchester United In The Sixties**	£12.99
0 233 99368 1	**Alex Ferguson: A Will to Win**	£6.99
0 233 99148 4	**David Beckham: My Story**	£12.99
0 233 99154 9	**Manchester United Official Review 97/98**	£9.99
0 233 99417 3	**The Official Manchester United Quiz Book**	£9.99
0 233 99216 2	**Manchester United Diary 1999**	£4.99
0 233 99498 X	**For Club and Country by Gary and Phil Neville**	£6.99
0 233 99155 7	**The Official Manchester United Illustrated Encyclopedia**	£25.00
0 233 99153 0	**Access All Areas: Behind the Scenes at Manchester United**	£14.99
0 233 99369 X	**Red and Raw: A Post-War History of Manchester United v Liverpool**	£14.99

For Children:

0 233 99373 8	**Old Trafford: Behind The Scenes**	£4.99
0 233 99218 9	**The Official Manchester United Annual 1999**	£5.75
0 233 99371 1	**Manchester United: Life On The Squad**	£4.99
0 233 99370 3	**Manchester United: Great Moments**	£4.99
0 233 99372 X	**Manchester United: Meet The Players**	£4.99
0 233 99374 6	**The Official Manchester United Log Book**	£4.99